JAPANESE GOVERNMENT LEADERSHIP AND MANAGEMENT

Japanese Government Leadership and Management

Charles F. Bingman
*School of Government and
Business Administration
The George Washington University*

St. Martin's Press   New York

First published in the United States of America in 1989

Printed in Hong Kong

ISBN 0–312–01181–4

Library of Congress Cataloging-in-Publication Data
Bingman, Charles F., 1929–
Japanese government leadership and management.

Bibliography: p.
Includes index.
1. Japan—Politics and government—1945–
2. Central–local government relations—Japan.
3. Industry and state—Japan. 4. Education and state—
Japan.   I. Title.
JQ1624.B56 1988   320.452   88–3162
ISBN 0–312–01181–4

Contents

Preface

Much is being written these days about Japanese private sector management, and these books and articles are creating a rich source of knowledge and understanding about how Japanese companies have achieved some remarkable successes.

There is, however, an even greater story to tell.

During a remarkable 20-year period after the end of World War II, the Japanese rewrote their Constitution; restructured the entire institutional architecture of their national, prefectural and municipal governments; redesigned their political and public administrative institutions and systems; and created a broad range of new programs for education, social service, and income security.

The Japanese had already known how to develop powerful industrial/commercial corporations. What has been even more challenging has been to find a way to provide responsible, responsive, and democratic government for its people — while simultaneously committing the government and the people to an alliance with private sector business for a "fast track" program of economic growth and sophistication.

The Japanese have clearly been very successful in these purposes. But the world seems slow in recognizing the achievements of the Japanese government in these successes, and there is an unfortunate shortage of good assessment available in English about the Japanese government, how it functions, what it has sought to accomplish, and how well it has done. This book is an attempt to help fill that gap.

My own background has been as a federal government executive — in the National Aeronautics and Space Administration, the Office of Management and Budget, and the Department of Transportation — and as a professor of public administration. My interests, therefore, are about how governments really work. This book is intended to provide a general picture of how Japanese governments at all levels function: what they do, how they do it, and how they finance themselves. It is aimed at all kinds of people who would benefit from that kind of understanding; not just scholars, but legislators, public officials, businessmen, international lawyers, and others who may find themselves needing to know more about Japan, and who will come to realize that you can't understand modern Japan without understanding its governments.

I gratefully acknowledge the help of several organizations. In 1982, I was sponsored in a research trip to Japan by the Council for International Urban Liaison and its research director, George G. Wynne, to study issues of Japanese government productivity and workforce management. Some of the material in this book, especially in Chapter 11 on public corporations, and portions of Chapter 2 on the Management and Coordination Agency and its staffing and control system, were originally published for CIUL. I also received help and encouragement from the American Consortium for International Public Administration and its staff director, John Magruder. During this period, I was associated with the National Academy of Public Administration, whose then President, J. Jackson Walter allowed me time to do research in Japan and writing in the back room.

Most of all, I wish to acknowledge two splendid Japanese organizations. The first is the General Center for Local Autonomy (the Jichi Sogo Center), and its International Programs Director, Mr Nobuharu Uyeno, who made extraordinary efforts to give me opportunities to meet key people at all levels of Japanese government, and to furnish me with many published materials in English which are not available in the United States. In addition, I am grateful for the opportunity to have met with Mr Keiichi Sato, then Chairman of the Institute of Administrative Management, and others of his staff who helped me with meetings, written material, and many valuable insights.

I know that this book only scratches the surface. I hope that it will help to generate a wider desire to know more about what I have come to believe is a remarkable experience in public management.

1 The Basic Structures and Concepts of the Japanese Government

In 1889, a new Japanese government was constituted out of a period of turmoil in which the power of the Emperor had been dissipated, and feudal lords had divided and all but ruined the country. At that time, Japan's first Constitution, called the Meiji Constitution, was created, and it restored the Emperor to the position of central, divine, and authoritarian power, and defined the government as subject to his will and the instrument of his authority.

This government became an autocratic instrument, patterned in large part on the Prussian model which was much admired by the aristocracy and the military who felt the pull of the old feudal traditions. During the next 50 years, the government aimed at the rapid development of the Japanese nation, its modernization, and its economic strength. The government's strengths lay in its ability to concentrate on these national priorities and force the pace of change in reasonably coherent ways. Its weaknesses were that it undervalued the rights of individuals, and failed adequately to deal with many pressing social issues that competed with its central priorities. In addition, the concentration of power at the national level led to costly neglect of governments at sub-national levels.

Despite the intent of the 1889 Constitution, the Emperor fell once again into a position as figurehead, and the real authority was increasingly exercised by powerful groups of government, military, and industrial leaders, working through the Cabinet. It was this concentration of power which, when taken over by militant nationalistic leaders, precipitated a Japanese policy of aggression that led to the invasion of China and the attack on Pearl Harbor which put Japan at war with the United States and half of the rest of the world.

World War II was a political, economic, and humane disaster for Japan. After the war, the Japanese people and leadership were faced with the extraordinary problems of rebuilding their nation, but it was widely recognized that they would not and could not do so under the old concepts of government. New concepts had rapidly to be created which set forth more effective answers about the role of governments and how governments should function. During this period, Japan was under the military government of the allied nations, and the Supreme Allied Commander, General Douglas MacArthur, had been tasked with making Japan a "democratic nation", as a condition of the termination of the allied occupation.

The Japanese Diet was laboring to draft a new constitution, as were many groups in the country, and in this conceptual process, the American occupation government was to play a crucial role. In March of 1946, the occupation government prepared its own draft of a constitution and submitted it informally to the Japanese Cabinet. It was this document that, with some modifications, became the vehicle for subsequent debate in the Diet and the country. In November of 1946, something very much like this draft was formally enacted and promulgated by the Emperor, taking effect in May of 1947.

CONSTITUTIONAL CONCEPTS OF GOVERNMENT

The Constitution which emerged is an extraordinary blend of the American and British political and public administration experience. In effect, it is American in spirit and British in its parliamentary structure and the role of the Emperor as symbolic head of a constitutional monarchy. But it can also be said that the implementation of the Constitution has become very Japanese.

The Emperor remains on a dynastic throne as "symbol of the State". He has no real power with respect to the functions of government. He is the final authority for many of the most important actions of government, but all of his actions must be taken "with the advice and approval of the Cabinet". He appoints the Prime Minister and the Chief Judge of the Supreme Court, and attests to the appointment of the principal Ministers of State. He formally convenes the Diet, and may dissolve the dominant House of Representatives and call for general elections. He accredits ambassadors, signs treaties, and promulgates laws, Cabinet orders, and amendments to the Constitution. But he no longer reigns as the supreme authority of the State. That role is now embodied in the Constitution which declares itself to be "the supreme law of the nation".

This new Constitution made many fundamental advances beyond the old Meiji Constitution of 1889:

1. It created a government intended to serve the Japanese people and not the Emperor or an aristocratic elite. Indeed, the Constitution begins by saying "We, the Japanese people, . . . ".

2. It retained the two Houses of the Diet, but gave the House of Representatives a superior position over the House of Councillors on most important matters, and sought to make it more democratic and responsible to the people by requiring more frequent elections.

3. It created a more representative parliamentary government on the British model and concentrated executive power in a Cabinet where the Prime Minister and at least half of the Ministers must be members of the Diet.

4. It created an independent judiciary.

5. It made constitutional provision for autonomous local governments in a structure of prefects and municipalities which have equal constitutional stature with the national government.

6. It places great emphasis — as much as any constitution in the world — on the civil and social rights of Japanese citizens, and requires that "the State shall use its endeavors for the promotion and extension of social welfare and security, and of the public health".

7. It makes a deliberate statement of the obligation of public officials: "all public officials are servants of the whole community, and not of any group thereof "; and "the people have a right to choose and dismiss their public officials".

8. It declares that all citizens are equal under the law; that there shall be no discrimination, and citizens are assured of a legal system which protects them against such abuses as improper arrest, illegal search or seizure, or improper seizure of property.

9. Citizens are assured freedom of thought, religion, speech and assembly, movement, and peaceful petition of redress against government actions.

10. Important social benefits are also mandated, including the right to a free "ordinary" (high school) education, and the right to work, which specifically includes the right to collective bargaining with wages, benefits, and working conditions fixed by law.

11. The Constitution places obligations on citizens. Each is required to support the Constitution by "the constant endeavor of the people, who shall refrain from any abuse of these freedoms and rights and shall always be responsible for utilizing them for the public welfare".

12. Finally, the Constitution makes an extraordinary renunciation of war which deserves to be quoted in full:

> Aspiring sincerely to an international peace based on justice and order, the Japanese people forever renounce war as a sovereign right of the nation and the threat or use of force as a means of settling international disputes.
>
> In order to accomplish the aim of the preceding paragraph, land, sea, and air forces, as well as other war potential, will never be maintained. The right of belligerency of the state will not be recognized.

The full text of the Constitution is included in this book as an Appendix.

Constitutional Stability

In the almost 40 years since its enactment, there has yet to be a formal motion in the Diet to amend the Constitution. It has been argued, then and now, that the Constitution was imposed by foreigners with foreign ideas which did not accord with Japanese character and tradition. And yet, whatever its genesis, the Constitution appears to have created satisfactory solutions to many of the serious flaws in Japanese government prior to World War II. The new Constitution makes it far more difficult for the government to fall into the hands of a power elite. It has created a real revolution in placing sovereign power in the hands of the people, and in enunciating in detail the imperatives of a genuinely democratic society. It deliberately relinquished centralist governmental power by providing for local government autonomy and creating a more effective framework of local governments to exercise that autonomy. And it charged public officials with the responsibility to be servants of the whole community, thus setting a new philosophical and ethical framework for the profession of public administration.

THE ROLE AND POWERS OF THE DIET

As defined in the Constitution, the Diet is responsible to the people as the sovereign power of the nation. It serves as "the highest organ of State power", and "the sole law-making organ of the State".

There are two Houses: the House of Representatives, and the House of Councillors, and members of both are elected by universal suffrage as representatives of the people.

The House of Representatives has been deliberately established as the superior body in many ways. Its 511 members are elected for four-year terms from 130 election districts. But because of the nature of the parliamentary system, members are seldom able to serve their full term.

The 252 members of the House of Councillors are elected for six-year terms by two different constituencies: 152 of them are elected in 47 districts which correspond to the 47 Japanese prefectures, and each prefecture elects two to eight members in proportion to their population; the other 100 members are members at large because they are chosen in general nation-wide elections. The theory is that Councillors will therefore be more statesmanlike since they are less beholden to narrow constituencies, but in fact, the real power base, even for the generally elected members is the same as for other elections, and the composition of the House of Councillors closely parallels that of the House of Representatives.

The exact number of members of either House is defined not by the Constitution, but by law, along with the definition of the electoral districts, and the groundrules for methods of voting and the conduct of elections.

The Constitution requires that the Diet conduct at least one "ordinary session" each year, but also provides that the Cabinet may convene extraordinary sessions, either by its own decision or by demand of one-fourth of the members of the House of Representatives. The ordinary session normally starts in mid-December, and in simpler times, usually lasted about 150 days. But like most modern legislative bodies, the Diet is now in session most of the year.

Both Houses function through a combination of general parliamentary debate on the floor in the British tradition, and through a set of about 16 standing committees in the American congressional style. Each House is free to appoint its own presiding officers and establish its own rules. Most legislation is decided by simple majority of members present, with certain exceptions defined by the Constitution which will be discussed later.

One of the most significant of the Constitutional powers of the Diet is the appointment of the Prime Minister, who, in turn, appoints the principal Ministers of State. The Constitution also requires that the Prime Minister and at least half of the Cabinet come from either

House of the Diet, and that "The Cabinet, in the exercise of executive power, shall be collectively responsible to the Diet." Thus, there is no separation of powers doctrine as in the United States.

The Prime Minister is empowered to dissolve the House of Representatives, essentially when he chooses, and precipitate new general elections. The House of Representatives in turn can upset the government by a vote of no confidence, or by rejection of a vote of confidence. If this happens, the Cabinet must resign within ten days, unless the Prime Minister dissolves the House of Representatives first. In any event, a general election must take place, and if the Cabinet has not already resigned, it must do so *en masse* after the election. It is this process which accounts for one of the most important elements of Japanese government — the instability and short-term service of its political leadership. Few House of Representatives members have ever served out their four-year terms, and sessions have been as short as six months. The average lifespan of Cabinets has, for various political reasons, been about nine months. This has important implications both in terms of the functioning of the Diet, and the long-term ascendency of the career bureaucracy in the executive ministries.

The House of Representatives has been given other powers in the legislative process which permit it to dominate the House of Councillors. As stated in the Constitution:

> A bill which is passed by the House of Representatives, and upon which the House of Councillors makes a decision different from that of the House of Representatives, becomes law when passed a second time by the House of Representatives by a majority of two-thirds or more of the members present.

This provision also applies if the House of Councillors fails to act at all. Similarly, all budget bills must be submitted by the Cabinet first to the House of Representatives; and if the House of Councillors fails to agree with the Representatives' bill, or fails to act on it within 30 days, "the decision of the House of Representatives shall be the decision of the Diet". These same procedures are also applicable to the ratification of treaties, and the appointment of the Prime Minister.

While this discussion lays out the basic framework of the Diet, it says little about the far more interesting issues of how the Diet really functions. But before that question can be effectively addressed, it is absolutely necessary to insert a discussion of the role of Japanese political parties, because the functioning of the parties is inextricably intertwined with the functioning of the Diet itself, and of the ministries of the executive branch of the government to a degree which is unparalleled in the American experience.

THE ROLE OF POLITICAL PARTIES

World War II was also a watershed in the redefinition of Japanese political parties. What emerged was not a two-party system, but a range of parties from communist and socialist to the ultra conservative vestiges of pre-war elites. Various consolidations took place, primarily in the mid-1950s as the Japanese tried to sort out their own political mainstreams. In brief, the current main parties are described below.

The Liberal Democratic Party (LDP)

The new LDP emerged almost immediately after the creation of the new Constitution as the dominant party in Japan, a position which, except for a brief nine-month period of 1947–8, it has never relinquished. The LDP is generally perceived to be the party of big business and agriculture, and while its real base is much broader, the backing and financial support of those interests have been the backbone of the party for almost 40 years of political dominance.

The New Liberal Club (NLC)

This small party was formed in 1976 as a split-off from the LDP, and was expected at that time to become the nucleus for a new party, but that has never happened. When the split occurred, its leaders sought a position of greater political flexibility and "morality". In recent years, however, it has most often found itself in alliance with the LDP, and its small (15–20) membership in the Diet has often been of real value to the LDP in maintaining its majority position. Finally, following the election landslide of the LDP in July of 1986, the NLC decided to disband and merge again with the LDP.

The Japan Socialist Party (JSP)

In 1955, two socialist parties combined to form the JSP which peaked in 1958 at about one-third of the popular vote in national elections, and 36% of the seats in the Diet. Since then, it has declined to about 25% of the membership, but it remains the second leading party in numbers and usually in influence. The JSP is very zealous in the pursuit of a socialist philosophy in the European tradition, and it relies heavily on the Solyo union — a left-wing confederation of unions with more than four million members, many of whom work for national or local governments or government corporations such as railroads and telecommunications.

The Democratic Socialist Party (DSP)

In 1960, the right wing of the JSP split away to form the DSP. It positions itself in the middle ground between the more militant JSP and the LDP, and has been holding about 30 seats in the Diet. Its major backing also comes from organized labor, but more from large industrial unions and urban constituencies.

The Clean Government Party (CGP)

Originally created to be the political arm of a major Buddhist religious sect with more than 16 million members, the CGP reorganized in 1962 to establish itself as a secular party seeking broader populist appeal, and in 1972 it terminated its official relationships with the Buddhist group. It has been able to seat 50–60 members in the Diet and make itself the third largest party in terms of membership. It has never fully divorced itself from its religious backing, but it has achieved a broader, very "neighborhood" grass-roots outreach through a network of local offices, student groups, community groups, and other interest affiliations. As its name suggests, it has adopted a position of advocating the need for "purification" of politics, government prudence and economy, and more programs for the disadvantaged in Japanese society.

The Japan Communist Party (JCP)

A post-war party, the JCP seriously hurt its standing with the Japanese public by falling under the influence first of the Soviet, and later of the Chinese communist parties, and it had a hard time defending world communism at home. After 1960 it changed its tactics to become more of a domestic party and tried for a broad mass appeal, with occasional real strength at the local government level where it concentrated on important local issues. Nationally, it has never done better than 6–10% of the popular vote and 15–20 members in the Diet. It has consistently advocated positions of hostility to the United States, and nationalization of many key industries, and neither position has helped its credibility.

Despite the existence of these six parties, and their varying fortunes over 40 years, the remarkable reality of Japanese politics is that it has had only one ruling party — the Liberal Democratic Party — which has controlled the Diet, the Cabinet, and political life in general during the entire post-war period. The reality is that Japanese politics is "the LDP vs. everybody else". Only the LDP has succeeded in pursuing a political course of action which has produced broad-based support. But the other parties share responsibility for this reality as well. None has proved flexible enough, or been willing enough to compromise its basic political position to build the kind of broad national support which would have been needed to challenge LDP supremacy. The JCP and the JSP have been fiercely doctrinaire, and the JSP and the DSP are seen as too reliant on their narrow union bases, and too opposed to the very "capitalist" elements which have made the Japanese economy the pride of its people and the envy of the industrial world. Thus, even when the LDP is distrusted, or seen as reactionary, or wrong on issues, most Japanese citizens appear to care even less for the alternatives and prefer to leverage the LDP.

All Japanese parties not excluding the communists attempt to sublimate within their ranks a wide and very diffuse range of interests, and each is famous — or infamous — for its intense internal infighting. Thus, the politics of "factions" is an important element of how party decisions are made; and in the case of the LDP, how national government decisions are made.

In all parties, but particularly in the LDP, factions form around personalities — usually senior experienced professional politicians with networks of supporters at all levels, and links with reliable sources of funds to finance enormously costly political campaigns and an expensive party apparatus. In truth, these linkages seem more important than a large party membership (even the LDP has fewer than 1,200,000 members out of a national population of 120,000,000), or even party stances on major policy issues. Japanese political leaders are not typically the popular, charismatic types seen in the US; they are hard-working, hard-bargaining political professionals who build backing through political skill, financial support, and an array of useful well positioned backers in the Diet and the bureaucracy, many of whom hitch their wagons to some rising star in furtherance of their own political ambitions and careers.

The LDP particularly seems to have mastered this style. Its political position at any given time is not so much driven by doctrine or ideology, as with the communists and socialists, but by a hard, pragmatic coalition of interests and individuals. Leaders rise to the top of the party by putting together coalitions of "factions". The party is a kaleidoscope of factions and interests within factions, and the pattern of the kaleidoscope and the balance of power is constantly shifting as leaders rise and fall, issues change, and backers reposition themselves.

One final note about the LDP is imperative. The man (there are few women in this upper political arena[1]) who rises to become President of the Liberal Democratic Party is almost certainly going to become the Prime Minister of Japan. The President is elected by the party every three years at its national conference. A President may serve two terms, but election for a third term would require an almost impossible two-thirds vote of the party's Diet members. (Yet in fact, Prime Minister Nakasone won such an extraordinary extension for a period of one year in September 1986.) While this election is ostensibly performed by the party conference, with its large representative membership, in fact, it is largely a *pro forma* ratification of a decision made by the party inner elite. Thus, the back room nature of party inner leadership and its influence on the affairs of government becomes obvious.

HOW THE DIET FUNCTIONS: THE THREE RINGS OF POWER

For many years, a popular US beer had as its symbol three intersecting and overlapping rings thus:

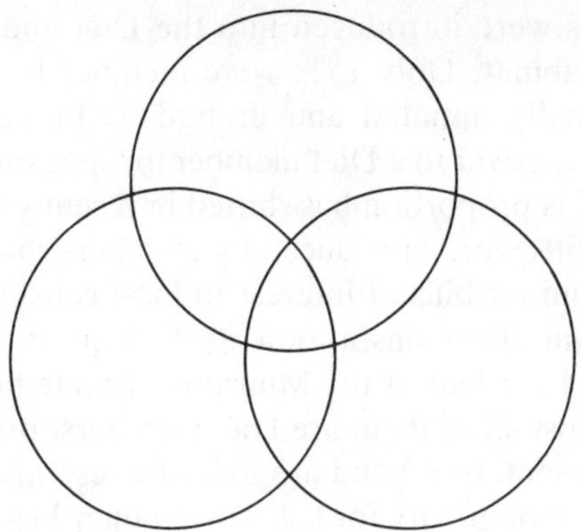

It is not clear what this signified to beer drinkers, but it is not a bad kind of symbol to explain how power in the Japanese political system works. The three rings of power in Japan are the Diet, the Liberal Democratic Party, and the ministries of the national government. Each of these circles has its broader affairs, but each is essentially structured to focus its power on the hot spot of public policy formulation where their roles intersect.

A case can be made that the weakest of these rings is the Diet itself, but the most useful perception is that the key people in each of these rings of power are very often the **same people**, serving three roles, and in the center of these three rings. It is almost impossible to know which role is being played, and which circle predominates. This can perhaps best be illustrated by a closer look at two of the key political processes which take place at the center of this power base — the legislative policy formulation process, and the approval of the budget for the national government.

The Legislative Process

Considered from the vantage point of the US Congress, the role of the Japanese Diet must appear to be singularly weak. Since the House of Representatives is clearly the most important body, most of this discussion will concentrate on how it functions. Contrary to US congressional experience, most proposed legislation originates not in the Diet itself, but from the ministries, through the Cabinet. A survey by Professor T. J. Pempel of the 5,501 bills enacted by the Diet between its first session in 1946 and its 76th in 1975 demonstrated that

85% of the bills were introduced into the Diet and officially sponsored by the Cabinet. Only 15% were member bills, and many of these were actually initiated and drafted by bureaucrats or party sources and turned over to a Diet member for sponsorship and formal introduction. This proportion has shifted in recent years, and in 1980 about 45% of bills were introduced by members, but many of these still tend to be minor bills of interest to local constituencies.

But recall that the Constitution itself requires that the Prime Minister and at least half of the Ministers of State be Diet members (in practice almost all of them are Diet members, primarily from the House of Representatives) and are formally responsible to the Diet. So the real center of gravity for legislative policy lies in the ministries and the question becomes who defines and initiates this flow.

The answer seems to be three-fold. Most initiatives are generated by the highly competent professional and technical staffs of career officials in the ministries, reflecting their official views about what is required. This flow is modulated by the policy initiatives of the political ministers who represent the policies of the current Prime Minister. But, as will be discussed later, these political appointees are short-timers and they seldom get a real grip on the affairs of their own ministries. The more vigorous and effective of them will see to it that the key bills will come close to implementation of the Cabinet's policy initiatives, and they can preclude bills which run counter to these initiatives, but for the bulk of the legislative flow, they simply lack the time and the personal staff resources to be of much influence, and the career bureaucracy is paramount.

Similarly, the parties attempt to influence this stream of legislative proposals within the ministries as bills are being prepared for submission for Cabinet consideration, and often the parties — or at least the LDP — can sway a decision and get what they want. But it is still a process controlled by the professional staff. The LDP has a second major opportunity to exercise its influence at the Cabinet level, and it must be said that if the LDP doesn't want a proposal to advance, it probably won't.

A look at the mechanisms for policy formulation of the Liberal Democratic Party will illustrate this process. The foremost official of the LDP is its President. When he is elected, he almost automatically becomes his party's candidate for Prime Minister, and this automatically assures his election by the Diet. The party also has an Executive Committee of about 30 members, and a powerful legislative arm called the Policy Affairs Research Council (PARC). All

LDP members of the Diet are automatically members of PARC.

PARC is the rather sophisticated mechanism for assembling and negotiating the policy positions of the LDP and lobbying the ministries, the Cabinet, and the Diet to gain acceptance of the party's views. It has about 18 standing committees, approximately structured to parallel both the major ministries of the government, and the major standing committees of the House of Representatives. Within the Diet, the majority LDP has the privilege of having one of its members heading each of the standing committees; and these and other Diet members are also semi-permanent members of the comparable standing committees of PARC.

The practical consequence of this whole complex process seems to be that the bureaucracy initiates the major portion of the legislative initiatives and represents the professional and technical expertise about public programs and the needs of the whole governmental structure down through the prefectures to municipal governments and their constituent interests. The LDP represents its own views, acting as a major broker to deal with client interests on specifics and negotiating out a position which balances the demands of the client groups and the conflicts of its own factions. When this position is developed, it is negotiated with the ministries, with final resolutions by the Prime Minister and the Cabinet. The Diet as an institution has little impact on this process, except through its members who have a role in these other circles.

When the Cabinet finally approves its legislative agenda, the battle is practically over. Both the party and the bureaucracy now have a vested interest in stewarding the agenda through the Diet with as little change as possible, and that is exactly what they do. The LDP now uses its Diet members to introduce bills, move them swiftly to a vote, and beat off opposition or change. While Diet members and their standing committees do have staffs, they are most often used for client services in the ministries, and are not particularly skilled in legislative policy matters. In fact, it is the professional career staff of the ministries, rather than the Diet staff, which shepherds bills through the legislative process. Party discipline is harsh and unyielding, and bad things can happen to party members who do not fall into line.

Client and lobbying groups clearly have a difficult time penetrating this process. The LDP has made efforts to become the principal source of client satisfaction. In contrast to US parties, the LDP maintains a strong base of permanent field offices which solicit the views of lobbyists and amalgamate them into its own policy formulation process. Ministries also deal directly with client interests but somewhat more defensively. Individual Diet members are highly sensitive to these client interests and often become advocates in the unfolding of the power brokerage process, but often on rather minor or parochial matters.

The potentials for influencing legislative policy are even worse for the opposition parties, and in fact their most effective role seems to be one of loud public debate and criticism aimed at the LDP rather than the Diet or the ministries. With a perpetual majority in the Diet, and a stranglehold on the policy formulation process, the LDP needs to make few compromises with minority parties. Both the Japan Communist Party and the Japan Socialist Party have contributed to their own difficulties by insisting on adhering closely and purely to their main ideological base and being relatively unwilling to negotiate and compromise.

The Diet and the Budget

A more technical discussion of the government's budget formulation process will be found in Chapter 4. It is important to note here that this process is driven by the Ministry of Finance (MOF) on behalf of the Cabinet and, after arduous negotiations and compromises with the ministries, it submits a proposed budget to the Cabinet in early January of each year. At the same time, the MOF sends the final proposals to the ministries and to all of the political parties.

Cabinet Ministers who feel that they lost an important decision can argue the toss one more time with the Cabinet through what is known as "restoration requests". These are few, and not usually on major items, since arguing major issues this late in the game simply isn't done. A small "reserve" is set aside in advance by the MOF so that money is not a factor and reclamas can be argued on their merits.

At the same time, the LDP reviews the proposed budget and decides whether it too wishes to reclama. The final decision is made in the residence of the Prime Minister in what must be fascinating political meetings, since the Cabinet, the Minister of Finance, and the top people of the LDP are all present! And yet, it appears that the agenda is predominantly rather small matters which are useful to reward or assuage some political interests rather than major challenges to the excruciatingly crafted budget proposals.

After this meeting in the Prime Minister's residence, the Cabinet almost immediately submits the officially approved budget to the Diet. This culminating process appears to have achieved some shift of budget influence away from the MOF and the ministries. The Prime Minister, however, really only considers from the party those items which are carefully identified in advance as "political", and might be known in US parlance as "pork": a bridge, a road, a hospital, help for a client group, or for a specific city or town. These final deals are generally not costly in total budget terms, and they lubricate the final stages of the budget conflict and sweeten the mood of the party for the ensuing action in the Diet.

The practical outcomes of this process have been exceptional, in that the Diet simply does not ever upset these results. In the period of 1955 through 1977, for example, the Diet made **only one substantive revision in the government's budget**! This kind of outcome can be very disturbing to those who are strong believers in the US constitutional separation of powers. The ministries do provide a good long-term stable and coordinated basis of policy formulation, planning and program implementation, free of much of the intervention by the Congress which weakens these capacities in the executive branch departments. In Japan, this is generally regarded as a valuable strength because it is seen as rational, stable, and comprehensive planning which permits all national interests to understand and to respond.

There is a growing feeling, however, that the role of the Diet as conceived by the Constitution has never been fully achieved, and that too much has been conceded to the Liberal Democratic Party. The impact of the Diet is seen often as petty and inconclusive, and while the LDP is generally responsible, the current system tends to use the official processes of government to freeze out political opposition or even consideration of feasible options. It can be argued, as it is in the United States, that the full democratic value of the legislative body cannot be realized unless and until it can provide strong national policy guidance, both in legislation and in the formulation of the national budget.

Note

1.   Shortly after this was written, the Japan Socialist Party elected Tohako Doi as its new chairwoman. See *Japan Times Weekly*, Vol. 26, No. 38, September 28, 1986.

2 The Prime Minister, the Cabinet, and the Central Agencies

To examine the role of the Japanese Prime Minister is to examine the exercise of central political power. Who runs Japan? The answer varies with time, events, and personalities, but without doubt, the central figure since World War II and before has been the Prime Minister, and the central instrument has been the Cabinet.

The Prime Minister is at the center of the three rings of power. First, the Prime Minister begins as the elected President of the Liberal Democratic Party, and is therefore the leader of the party which has ruled Japan for an unbroken period of 40 years. Second, the PM is elected to office by the Diet, and while he and the full Cabinet are thus responsible to the Diet they are also powerful insiders in the Diet's deliberations. Third, the PM becomes the center of power as the leader of the executive ministries of government, which gives him the potential to direct and command the organizations and people who do the bulk of the planning and implementation of public programs.

These three relationships seem to give the Prime Minister a position of unparalleled power. But in fact each is a relationship which works in both directions. As President of the party, the PM exerts great influence on it; but at the same time, the party expects and demands that he will see to its interests as PM. While the PM and the Cabinet are constitutionally accountable to the Diet, he can turn this around and use his parliamentary presence and that of the other Cabinet members to influence and persuade from the inside. And, while the Cabinet constitutes the layer of political leadership which supposedly directs and supervises the ministries, that layer is very thin and is seldom a match for the skilled and experienced permanent career staff.

The Japanese Constitution provides that the Prime Minister be elected by the Diet from among its members, and for the Prime Minister to appoint not more than 20 Ministers of State, a majority of whom must also be Diet members from either House. In fact the Diet has almost always elected the President of the LDP; almost all, and not just half, of ministers have come from the Diet; most of them have come from the House of Representatives; and none have been members of opposition parties.

The Cabinet is a genuine collegial body. On the face of it, its members serve at the pleasure of the Prime Minister, and can be dismissed at his discretion. But at the same time, contrary to US experience, these are men who are also members of the Diet and have their own political "wheelbase" because they lead or represent the interest of important factions either in the Diet or in the party. The selection of Cabinet Ministers is best understood as a careful exercise in the balancing of these factional interests. This also helps to account for the fact that Ministers of State seldom serve for long periods. They are often appointed as a reward for faithful service, for supporting the administration in some crucial struggle, or for their ability to lead the ministry in pressing for an important but transient policy issue.

Nor does leaving the Cabinet carry much political stigma, and it certainly does not lead to removal from the political mainstream as it often does in the United States. Ex Cabinet Ministers retain their party and factional roles. Many move in and out of the Cabinet in the British tradition, never really out of power, but exercising their influence in different forums.

In fact, despite relatively brief stints in a given post, most Cabinet Ministers including Prime Ministers, are very experienced politicians. For the first 25 years of the post-war period, 46% of the appointed Ministers were career politicians, 18% were former career officials who won seats in the Diet, and the remaining 24% were experienced businessmen, lawyers, university professors, or journalists who acquired experience in, and a taste for, politics.

CABINET FUNCTIONS

Despite its somewhat transient membership (57% last less than one year, and 77% less than two), the Cabinet remains by design and in reality an extremely powerful body. The Prime Minister may dominate by his powers of leadership, and all votes of the Cabinet are, by tradition, expected to be unanimous, but the PM has only one vote, and decisions are arrived at by negotiation and compromise.

A formal summary of Cabinet authorities is an illuminating explanation of its power. The Constitution defines it as "the highest executive authority of the government". It formulates government policy and plans, directs the ministries of the government both individually and collectively, manages both domestic and foreign affairs, prepares the budget, administers the civil service, and submits proposed legislation to the Diet on behalf of the executive branch.

In addition, it issues Cabinet orders which have the force and effect of law, apppoints Justices of the Supreme Court, and is responsible for advising the Emperor as to the formal processes of calling the Diet into session, or dissolving it and calling for general elections.

The Cabinet has varied in size from 17 to its present number of 20. All are Ministers of State, and are collectively accountable to the Diet. Twelve hold portfolios as heads of the major ministries: Justice, Foreign Affairs, Finance, International Trade and Industry, Transportation, Labor, Education, Health and Welfare, Agriculture, Forestry and Fisheries, Posts and Telecommunications, Construction, and Home Affairs (see Organization Chart 1). The Prime Minister has some discretion as to how he allocates the other eight ministerial appointments. One is by law given to the Chief Secretary of the Cabinet, and the others are assigned among the nine "Prime Minister's agencies" shown on Organization Chart 2.

There have been a number of different motives which have led to the evolution of this peculiar collection of Prime Minister's agencies. A number of them are strictly to organize and administer the affairs of the Prime Minister and the Cabinet. The most important of these are the Cabinet Secretariat which organizes the agenda for Cabinet meetings, and provides research, data gathering, and policy advice to the Cabinet and liaison and communications throughout the government. The Chief Secretary of the Cabinet is usually a close political associate of the Prime Minister, and is influential in maintaining regular working relationships with the Liberal Democratic Party.

Also important is the Cabinet Legislative Bureau which prepares Cabinet legislation for submission to the Diet, coordinates the review and approval of legislation originating in the ministries, and negotiates legislative matters with the standing committees of the Diet. This Bureau also prepares and coordinates Cabinet Orders and refers them to the Cabinet for approval, along with the views of the relevant ministries.

The National Defense Council is a policy body similar in character to the National Security Council in the US government. It is chaired by the Prime Minister and its other members are the Director-General of the Defense Agency (which is in itself a part of the Prime

Organization
Chart 1

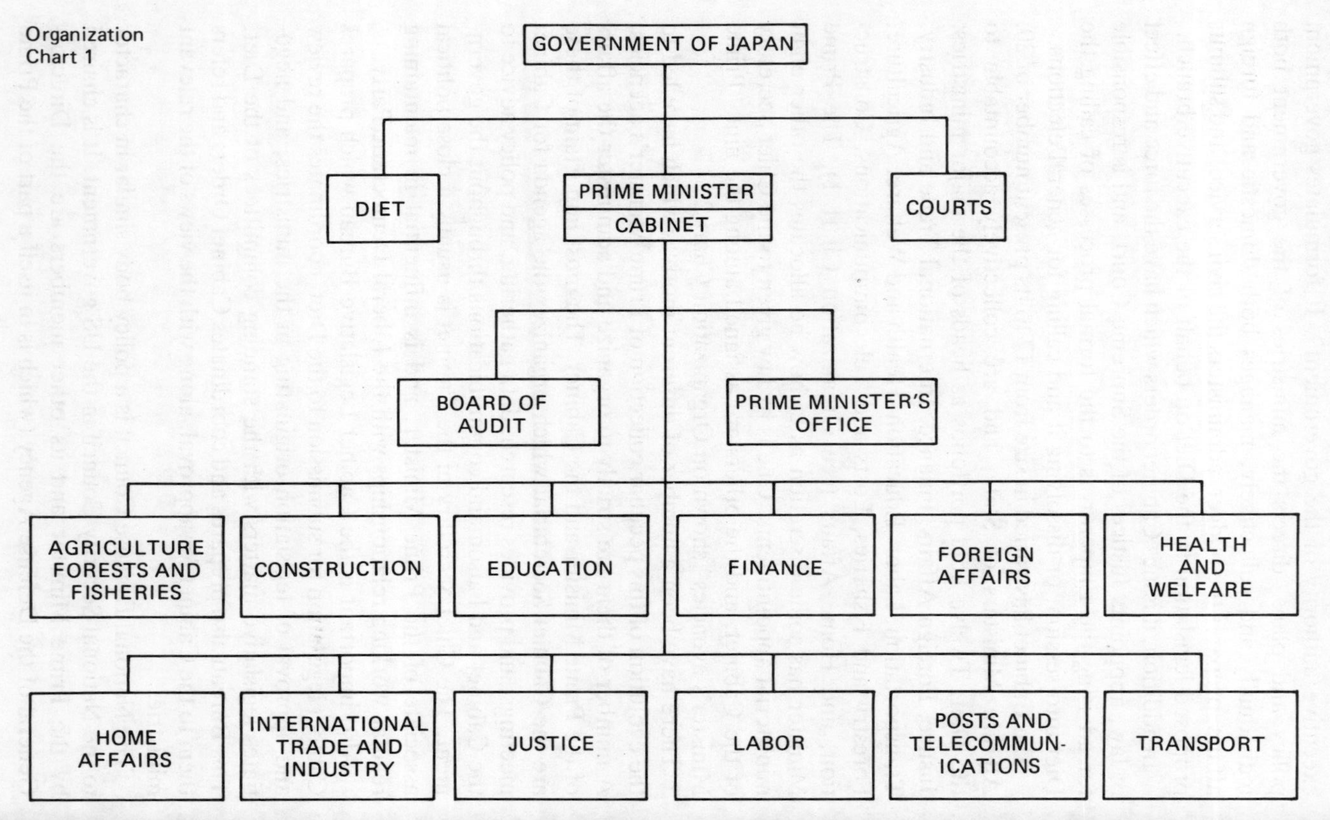

Organization
Chart 2

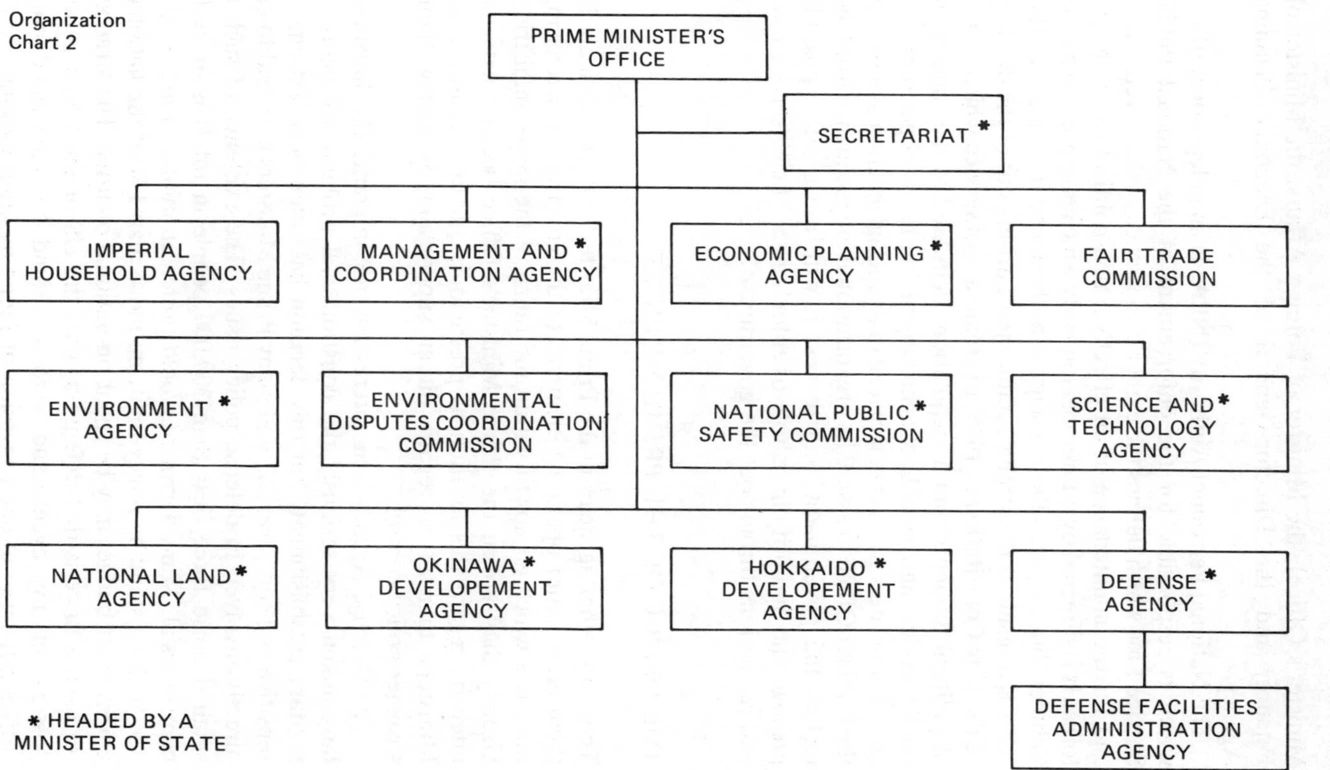

Minister's Office), the Minister of Foreign Affairs, the Minister of Finance, and the Director-General of the Economic Planning Agency.

The National Personnel Authority (NPA) is an independent office which is responsible for the enforcement of the National Public Service Law which defines the career civil service of the government; and for the maintenance of an effective, non-political career work-force. It is directed by a three-person body which is appointed by the Cabinet, but requires the consent of both Houses of the Diet. The NPA is a result of the strong commitment, arising out of the drafting of the new Constitution in 1946, to create a civil service which is free of political influence and manipulation, dedicated to the concept of public service, and capable of achieving higher levels of performance and effectiveness. It has been placed in its special location as a part of the Cabinet Office to assure its organizational independence from the rest of the government, and to vest it with the greatest possible prestige and authority in its role of enforcement of civil service laws and regulations throughout the government.

THE OFFICE OF THE PRIME MINISTER

There are other agencies in the Prime Minister's Office which are in themselves major operating elements of the government, exercising functions which do not fit within the range of the major ministries. Usually they are in the Prime Minister's Office because external interests regard this location as prestigious, and/or because Prime Ministers themselves regard direct supervision as giving them stronger policy control.

The Defense Agency is an interesting case in point. The Japanese have taken very seriously the constitutional prohibition against a military establishment, but this decision has often been extremely sensitive and controversial, and many Prime Ministers have had to be directly involved in defense policy issues. The existence of such a small defense force (less than 300,000 people in total) is in itself controversial. Many Japanese would prefer no military force at all, and by long-standing policy limit, no more than 1% of the national government budget may be spent on national security. The strategy for such a force is that defense against the US or the USSR is not possible in any event, and a force should be maintained only sufficiently large to deter invasion of Japan by other nations.

But this strategy makes Japan heavily dependent on its bilateral treaty of mutual defense with the United States which has become the shield against threats or attacks that are beyond the capacities of this wholly inadequate military establishment. Even if war or invasion are not likely, Japan is vulnerable to threats of blockade or embargos on imports such as oil and minerals on which Japan is so dependent, and it is the US which would have to come to the rescue.

In the immediate post-war period, Japan adopted a non-nuclear policy which it has staunchly maintained, and a position of strict neutrality which created serious opposition at that time to the US treaty. In the '60s and '70s, the Japan Communist Party advocated alliance first with the Soviets and then the Chinese, in preference to the American linkage. It was not until the late 1970s that public opinion settled down into general acceptance of the small defense force and the American security umbrella.

Two other elements of the Prime Minister's Office are of great importance — the Economic Planning Agency, and the Management and Coordination Agency.

The Economic Planning Agency

The Economic Planning Agency appears to have substantial acceptance because it is able to deal on a cooperative basis with the private sector and other government agencies to bring together the best economic forecasting information and produce credible economic planning frameworks. The agency is responsible for the information of basic "policy for the steering of the economy as a whole". To fulfil this charter, it produces a long-term general economic plan for the nation, and an annual economic program for the government. It is responsible for the coordination of economic and policy programs across the whole government on behalf of the Cabinet, and for the planning and coordination of international economic matters.

Japan does not have a managed economy in the socialist sense. Rather, it seeks to evolve a consensus among the important players as to what the economic future will be and what steps should be taken to meet that future. The Economic Planning Agency provides the kind of planning and analysis which provides targets for long-term economic development, and proposals or guidelines defining what would be necessary for balanced national development toward those targets. It provides standard economic indicators and economic assumptions which are used for both government and corporate planning. It draws attention to various national needs and trends, and how these will influence the economy. It will go so far as to develop basic price policies for segments of industry, and "designation of the reasonable standard and structure of living" for Japanese citizens. It works most closely with the Ministries of Finance and International Trade and Industry, and with the Bank of Japan, the Development Bank, and the Export–Import Bank.

Although the Economic Planning Agency is generally well regarded as a technical service, the recommendations of the recent final report of "The Provisional Commission on Administrative Reform" are revealing about the growing concern over the effectiveness of national economic planning. This Provisional Commission has been a major venture of the current and previous Prime Ministers, and its recommendations are important and widely accepted. The report reflects the growing belief that the days of exhilarating and almost automatic economic growth are over, and Japan's economic future will be far more troubled and uncertain than its past. Therefore, the report has recommended the establishment of a new "General Planning Council" as the capstone for the planning system. The Council would be in the Prime Minister's office, and would consist of fewer than ten experts from the private sector. The role of the Council would be to provide advice and guidance to the Cabinet on such issues as comprehensive perspectives for the future, measures to secure greater coordination of economic plans, appropriate national economic objectives, and better links between long-term and short-term economic planning.

This proposal appears to have three important objectives. First, it offers a new vehicle for the private sector to influence the formulation of national economic plans at the highest levels of government. Second, it creates a means for the Prime Minister and the Cabinet to get a stronger central grip on the constituent elements of planning throughout the government. And third, it would promote genuine improvements in the quality and comprehensiveness of planning work. The report cites the fact that many ministries do not now have really effective planning in their areas of influence. It also advocates that certain planning linkages be improved. For example, it points out that the huge public construction budget is regional or prefectural rather than national, and that science and technology planning is not linked to central planning assumptions.

There are references to the need to keep planning flexible. In other words, the report attractively advocates better and more comprehensive planning, longer time frames for planning, and better links between such comprehensive planning and short-term budget cycles, but it also recognizes that plans should not be developed which are so detailed that they become stultifying. But the real driving force behind these planning proposals is obviously the current serious budget deficit, and the feeling that some of this deficit can be attributed to the failure to rely on what might be called serious "technical" planning rather than the joys of political program enrichment.

The Management and Coordination Agency

The Management and Coordination Agency (MCA; until recently, the Administrative Management Agency) represents the "meat and potatoes" level of public administration. A simple recitation of its responsibilities can be counted on to produce instant drowsiness and a desire to think about something else. And yet, these functions are important ones, and their equivalents are found in every truly effective government in the world. The problem is that they are found in abundance in every truly miserable, bureaucratic government as well. Here is what the MCA does: it is responsible for the planning and development of basic administrative systems and procedures; it administers statutes which define the organization structure of ministries and agencies, and controls organization changes; it negotiates the staffing levels of ministries within ceilings defined in statute; and it exerts similar controls with respect to the structure and staffing of government corporations. In addition, the MCA sets the groundrules for the use of computers, data processing and office automation; concerns itself with the gathering and analysis of important statistical information, data bases, survey methods, and official statistical reports; and it performs inspections and evaluations of agency compliance with the requirements of these administrative systems. In carrying out this last responsibility, the MCA maintains a group of field offices throughout Japan which conduct audits and investigations which include those functions that are delegated by the national government for performance at the prefectural or municipal level.

It is revealing that the reputation of this Agency in the national government is very high. It apears that these responsibilities are taken seriously, and it has been important to recent Prime Ministers to back its authority; in fact, as the Japanese have increasingly fallen prey to the budget deficit ills which have plagued other governments, the stock of this organization has risen in value. It is not a contemptible assignment for rising politicians, and in fact, the present Prime Minister, Mr Yasuhiro Nakasone served a period of time as its Director-General. In this position, he became a key figure in the major administrative reform program which was one of the staples of his administration. It is a valuable assignment for top careerists, and a good place to master some of the technical intricacies of government management.

One of the key functions of the MCA in recent years has been that of staffing control, and it is worth an extended discussion of this function to illustrate the interplay between the Office of the Prime Minister and the rest of the government, and to introduce the reader to the concept of "scrap and build".

Staffing Control

Perhaps the single most compelling approach to the administrative control of the national government has been in the form of control over the size of the workforce. This approach has been used far more rationally than in the US federal government because it has been more frank and explicit in its objective, and less spastic and contradictory in its application.

The number of national public employees increased drastically from the end of World War II until the mid-1960s, driven by legitimate needs for expansion of public programs, but also by some euphoria reflecting this exceptional period of economic growth and national prosperity. But the Japanese were, for a complex set of reasons, not comfortable with this growth, and even before the energy crisis of the early 1970s, there was a consensus that the growth of government had to be constrained. After struggling with administrative controls for several years, the Diet in 1969 enacted the extraordinary Law Concerning the Fixed Number of Personnel of Administrative Organizations (referred to as the "Total Staff Number Law") which put a ceiling on the total population of civil servants in the regular ministries and agencies of the national government. Figure 2.1 dramatically shows the consequences of this "capping" of the workforce population.

The Total Staff Number Law has now been in continuous effect for more than 16 years and has caused a "zero sum game" to be forced on the ministerial establishment, administered by the MCA. Almost no

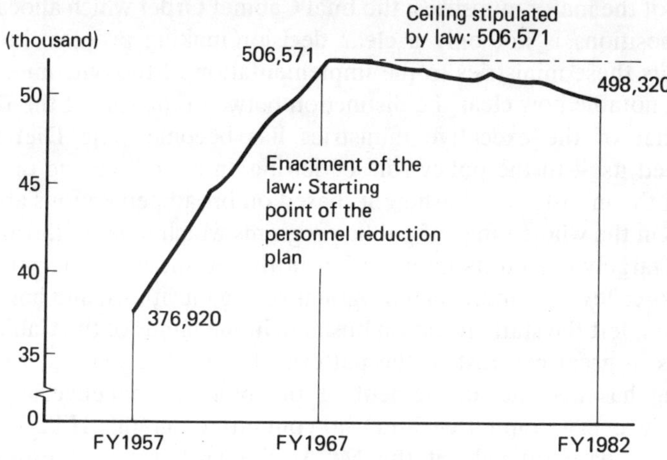

Figure 2.1: Number of National Public Employees

agency has been static during this period, but increases which have been permitted in some activities have had to be matched by comparable decreases in others. For example, the Ministry of Education increased by almost 28,000 in order to build up nationally operated universities and technical schools; but the Ministry of Agriculture, Forestry and Fisheries shrank by 23,000, and Posts and Telecommunications by more than 9,000 during this same period. This need for zero sum outcome precipitated a series of six back-to-back "Personnel Reduction Plans" running from two to five years each. These efforts are not just arbitrary staff cutting exercises. Under the direction of the MCA, they are genuine workforce plans because there had to be a serious attempt to predict where the programs of the government would be changing in the near term future, and to estimate the workforce consequences of these changes, both up and down. The net results of these increases had to be measured to determine whether they could be kept within the statutorily mandated ceiling. If they could not, then a second round of negotiations was used by MCA to further squeeze the ministries.

The culmination of this process is a formal decision by the Cabinet which, as stated earlier, is a far more powerful decision-making body more on the lines of the British or Canadian models than its weak and ill-defined American counterpart. Since the Cabinet consists of the heads of the major ministries, the final Cabinet Order which allocates staff positions is not only a clear decision-making process, but it commits these ministries to the implementation of the outcome.

It is notable how clear the distinction between the role of the Diet and that of the executive ministries has become. The Diet has confined itself to the policy role of setting an overall ceiling on the size of the ministry establishment, based on broad perceptions about trends in the whole range of public programs which it has authorized. It has largely ceased its intervention in the business of determining workforce levels in individual programs or organizations, and has, for 16 years, left the staff allocation business in the hands of the Cabinet. This is in great contrast to the pattern of the US Congress, where staffing has become an element of the political maneuverings of virtually every committee and sub-committee on the Hill. In an interview with officials of the MCA, the author was questioned extensively about President Reagan's program to trim 75,000 employees from the Federal payroll and there was polite but clear amazement that a reduction of that size had already been achieved. These Japanese officials were well aware of the pattern of Congressional intervention in categorical staffing decisions and the difficulties which this presents to any President who is attempting a government-wide workforce control program.

The practical result of the Japanese approach to workforce control is, however, more subtle than this summary suggests. In reality, the workforce in the US executive branch has also been held to a plateau for many years. Federal employment has increased only 9.6% between 1952 and 1980 (2.5 million to 2.8 million), and while there were 163 federal employees per 10,000 US citizens in 1952, that ratio had declined to 125 per 10,000 in 1980. The difference lies in the fact that the Japanese approach is more "strategic" — a more deliberate comprehensive planning approach based on assessments of need; a greater ability to identify where staff cuts are possible, free from political "protectionism"; and greater flexibility to shift staffing positions to areas of greatest need without the protracted delays inherent in the legislative process. Also missing is much of the frustration which occurs because the executive branch has lost control of its own workforce decisions to the diffuse and uncoordinated actions of the Congress, which can and does involve itself in the most detailed levels of agency staffing.

The successive Personnel Reduction Plans directed by the Cabinet have required tough minded and difficult negotiations, but they have also provided a far greater degree of certainty against which future workforce plans can be made, and implementation undertaken. The US pattern has all but destroyed any incentive for agencies to plan and manage their workforces, since every year brings new uncertainties, and the combination of White House reviews and Congressional decisions can drastically change the results compared to what the agencies themselves had estimated. In the face of these uncertainties and changes, agencies are motivated to "game" their own numbers on the high side, and to play off the Congress against the White House, further adding to the confusion.

There are additional consequences which flow from Japan's total staffing control approach. It has apparently become a strong counter-force against the creation of new organizations, since the staff for any new entity, however small, must be gouged out of existing organizations. The government therefore has set a deliberate "scrap and build" policy under which a new bureau-level organization can be created only if another bureau is eliminated, recognizing that there is a direct link between new organizations and pressure for staff increases. As a result, the total numbers of bureaus has been stable at about 114 for several years, and new programs or functions tend to be placed within existing ministries or agencies. Since there has been tight control over the size of ministerial administrative overhead staffs, this tends to force their greater relative productivity.

One other consequence of this total staffing control system is highly relevant. It has, in its peculiarly governmental way, created "bottom line" motivations not unlike the profit and loss bottom line of private companies. That is, it appears to force motivations for **work-place effectiveness** throughout government. Ministries are constantly under the gun to find ways to trim workload requirements or to improve the efficiency of their own procedures in order to keep the work burden from overpowering the staff. This in turn has led to sympathetic reception of management improvement ideas, the introduction of labor-saving office automation, and the hand-off of certain work to the private sector. It has also apparently modulated to some degree the creation of regulations, licensing activities, or reporting requirements which are work-intensive to sustain.

The above discussion deals with the workforce controls which are applied by the Management and Coordination Agency to the government's regular ministries and bureaus. The Total Staff Number Law did not apply directly to the public corporations which the national government has created, but these corporations have not been exempt from the general policy of staffing control. Each personnel curtailment plan developed by the Cabinet has included staffing limits for corporations, including such large and important organizations as the Japanese National Railroads, and the Nippon Telegraph and Telephone Corporation. These corporations in total had, until recent reforms, 935,000 employees, which was three-fourths as large as the population of the regular ministries.

The Provisional Commission for Administrative Reform recommended that the old Administrative Management Agency be abolished, and the new Management and Coordination Agency be created, and this was among the first of the results of the Commission's proposals to be implemented by the Cabinet.

3 Exercising Central Government Authority: the Ministry of Finance

The essence of Japanese government authority can be perceived by understanding the Ministry of Finance (MOF) and how it functions. It is generally considered to be the single most powerful entity in the national government, and a coveted political post. It exerts its influence over all other ministries as a principal instrument of the Cabinet to press its policies and initiatives, and it is a powerful counterfoil to balance off the demands of the professional staffs of the other ministries, primarily through its control of the budget. This influence also extends down into prefectures and municipalities because of the heavy flow of funds from the national government, all of which must be approved by the Ministry of Finance.

Perhaps even more significant is MOF's role in the total Japanese economy, which is to say the heart of modern-day Japan. Japan has rather deliberately built a heavily integrated set of relationships between the central government and the private sector, including its all-powerful banks; and the key to this set of relationships is the MOF.

The ministry obviously functions within all of the constraints of the political system, but even the following straightforward description of its formal roles and authorities begins to convey the sense of power which it wields, and how that power is deployed.

1. The Ministry of Finance is essentially responsible for the design of the national tax system. It has the role and technical staff resources to develop tax system strategy, including decisions about how the tax structure can aid or hinder the private sector and individual citizens. It estimates tax revenues and formulates the basic economic assumptions on which both tax revenues and budget strategies are based. And it sets national policy with respect to the tax structures on which the revenues of local

governments are based, excluding the issuance of local municipal bonds.

2. It plans and operates the national financial system including broad financial planning, management of the national currency, control over the receipts and disbursements of the government, control of government investments, and the issuance of national bonds and treasury bills; and it is the administrator of the national debt.

   Actual collection of personal and corporate income taxes, property taxes, and such indirect taxes as the liquor tax is performed by the separate National Tax Administration Agency, much like its counterpart Internal Revenue Service in the US Treasury.

3. The MOF has enormous regulatory powers over the banking system. It supervises the Bank of Japan, which functions as the national central bank. It sets policies and regulations for all financial institutions, licences commercial banks and savings and loan companies, and exerts control over the interest rates charged by these institutions. It supervises the Deposit Insurance Organization and system, and finally, it is responsible for inspecting the operations of these institutions.

4. The Ministry of Finance also regulates the operation of securities trading. It licenses securities exchanges, securities companies, and investment companies. It supervises the trading of securities and registers and approves public offerings. In addition, MOF licenses insurance businesses, and it even sets standards for public accounting and auditing, and supervises the activities of certified public accountants.

5. Through its Customs and Tariff Bureau, MOF sets and collects customs duties, tonnage taxes, and fees on maritime shipping. It administers the customs system which involves policies and international customs and tariff agreements which define standards which must be met by foreign importers of goods into Japan; and it controls the operations of customs house brokers and bonding warehouses.

6. MOF plays a central role in international economic trade. In addition to customs and tariffs, it is the chief strategist and planner of international balance of trade issues, international monetary policy, and the issues of foreign investment in Japan. It directly supervises the Export–Import Bank, the Japan Investment Bank, and other government investment mechanisms in international trade.

7. Through its powerful Budget Bureau, MOF plans and executes the national government budget system and is the final co-ordinator, negotiator, and decision-maker on the budget short of the Cabinet. It prepares the formal Prime Minister's Budget for Cabinet approval and submission to the Diet.

The tax structure of Japanese governments is, predictably, complex and sophisticated at both the national and local government levels, and in keeping with its long history of centralist national power, the national government is a heavy financier for local governments and wields great influence over them as a consequence.

The main taxes levied by the national government (1985) are as follows:

1. *Individual income taxes*, which are levied on the net income of individuals and which produce about 39% of total tax revenues.
2. *Corporation taxes*, which are levied on the net income of businesses and produce about 32% of all taxes.
3. *The gasoline tax*, which is an indirect tax levied on gasoline shipped from refineries or withdrawn from bonded areas, and is from 4 to 5% of total tax revenue.
4. *The liquor tax*, which is an indirect tax on domestic liquors shipped from manufacturing premises, and on imported liquors withdrawn from bonded areas. It yields about 5% of the total.
5. *The commodity tax*, which is also an indirect tax levied on those who manufacture and sell certain kinds of commodities and yields almost 4% of taxes.
6. In addition, there is a wide range of other taxes including gift and inheritance taxes, and taxes on sugar, roads, aviation fuel, securities transactions, travel, stamps, and even playing cards. There are also customs duties, many licensing and registration fees, and tonnage taxes on cargo shipments and port usage. These taxes in total yield the remaining 15% of tax revenues.

For better than a decade, the national government has collected about 65% of all tax revenues, with prefectures and municipalities levying the rest. But there is also a series of transfer arrangements by which nationally collected revenue is transferred to both levels of local government. There is a National Subsidy, a Local Allocation Tax which consists of about 32% of the revenue from the national income tax, corporation tax and liquor tax; and there is the Local

Transfer Tax in which the national government collects localized taxes as a matter of convenience, and transfers the funds back. When the total effect of these transfers is taken into account, the actual tax revenue of the national government versus the local governments is closer to 50–50.

As local governments have been building up, these transfers have been rapidly growing as shown in Table 3.1:

Table 3.1:   National Funds Transferred
to Local Governments
(Billion Yen)

Year	Local Allocation	Local Transfer	National Subsidy	Total
1965	7.2	.5	10.9	18.6
1970	18.0	1.1	20.9	40.0
1975	33.5	2.5	58.8	94.8
1979	56.8	4.4	98.2	159.4

THE BANKING SYSTEM

The influence of the Ministry of Finance on the national banking system is very great, and perhaps can be better understood if the importance of the banks themselves is better understood. While the whole complex set of relationships which fuel economic development is extremely hard to understand from the outside, Drucker[1] points out that Japanese companies have relied less on issuing securities to obtain investment capital and more on borrowing from banks. In effect, banks provide funds which are technically business loans, but in fact constitute the major source of development capital for most companies. These bank loans are particularly important for new businesses and for those such as high technology firms where the capital investment is very large. These loans often give banks a controlling interest, or at least a strong voice in the management of companies. Japanese industry motives are first and foremost to maximize sales and cover the interest cost of capital supplied by the banks. Public holdings of corporate securities are kept as small as possible, and stockholders have relatively little say in corporate policy. Thus, the critical links are between corporate leadership, their bankers, and the Ministry of Finance.

TAX POLICIES

The structure of tax revenues relies heavily on direct taxes which are better than 73% of the total of all tax revenues. While the tax burden as a percentage of national revenue is rather low at 23.9% (1982), such direct and visible taxes have been increasing steadily since World War II (1950 = 55%) and have made the Japanese public very sensitive to, and very resistant to, further tax increases of this kind. At the same time, corporate taxes have been increasing as well, both in absolute terms because of the rapid growth of the Japanese economy, and in relative terms, showing the importance of corporations in the total Japanese economy. Starting in 1950, a new policy was introduced which reduced emphasis on indirect sources of income in favor of direct taxation. In 1960 a general policy was adopted to limit the total tax burden (exclusive of social security taxes) to about 20% of national income, and this limitation was roughly effective until the 1980s. In 1965 the national government issued bonds for the first time since the war as a Keynesian "countercyclical" policy measure. This new tool permitted unprecedented large-scale personal income tax reductions in 1966, which was politically attractive but helped put the Japanese government into the horrors of deficit financing from which it has yet to emerge.

INDIVIDUAL INCOME TAXES

In the fiscal year 1983 almost 41 million people, or almost 88% of the total number of individual wage and salary earners paid the national income tax. The individual income tax system is designed to be highly progressive; that is, the greater the person's income, the higher percentage of tax is paid. As in the American system, taxes are "self-assessed". But taxes on wages and salaries and on various forms of interest and dividends are withheld at the source, and in a unique feature, final adjustments are computed by companies between withheld amounts and the employees' final tax liability. Thus, unless these people have other reportable income, they are not required to file a tax return. In fact, so many people have their taxes settled in this effective manner that only seven million individual tax-payers filed returns in 1983.

The overall tax system is very comparable in design to that of the United States. It provides a series of provisions for a basic personal exemption, exemptions for spouses and dependents, special provisions for age, degrees of handicap, medical expenses, insurance costs, and losses from casualties. Income tax rates are graduated into 15 steps from the lowest of 10.5% for taxable income of 500,000 yen or less ($3125 at 160 yen to the dollar) to the highest of 70% for income over 80 million yen. Tax credits of from 5 to 10% are given for dividends; and for 18% of the annual house mortgage repayment up to certain limits.

The absolutely dominant fact of life in Japanese fiscal matters is the extraordinary resistance of the people to any threatened or potential increases in these personal income taxes. Even the very serious leveling off in the rate of growth of the economy has not weakened this resistance; in fact, personal income taxes have been **decreased** in 1971, 1973, 1974 (the largest in history), and again in 1983. Even more than in the United States, national tax policy has been driven by the political infeasibility of increasing personal taxes.

CORPORATION TAXES

During the post-war period, corporate taxes have been increasing both in absolute terms, because of the rapid growth of the economy, and in relative terms. Corporate income taxes (called corporation taxes) were just 14.7% of national tax revenues in 1950, but are now up to 42%. In international comparison, Japanese corporate taxes (income and profit only; local taxes included) were 19.6% of the total collected in 1983, compared to just 5.5% in the United States, 10.8% in the United Kingdom, and 4.3% in France.

But these figures by themselves are not fully explanatory. While they certainly say that corporations carry their own weight in financing the government, these same corporations have, especially since the war, enjoyed a very special relationship with the government, centering around a broad policy which has favored and supported expansion and development of many favored and priority industries which have fitted into a fairly well articulated national plan and strategy for the Japanese economy. It has been seen in the national interest to hold down corporate taxes wherever possible, and to grant certain tax advantages or subsidies to channel the evolution of the private sector in many ways. This led to a series of special laws during the '50s and '60s which conveyed tax advantages to favored industries. Many of these were originated by the Ministry of International Trade and Industry (MITI), which has seen its role as the formulator of this strategy along with leaders of the private sector. MITI has also been the principal advocate of these measures within the Cabinet and the Diet, even when it found itself in conflict with the Ministry of Finance, or of other ministries. Over the course of a number of years, advantages of the following kinds have been authorized:

1. Specific tax exemptions for favored industries.
2. Rapid amortization for research and development investments.
3. Government loans at subsidized interest rates.
4. Reevaluation of "inflated" assets.
5. Exemptions of up to 80% on income from exports.
6. Exemptions from tariffs on critical imports (i.e. technology, machinery, critical materials such as petrochemical feed materials).
7. Tax exemptions for industrial relocation.
8. Permission to create special tax exempt "reserves" for special purposes.
9. Tax payment deferrals.
10. Elimination of commodity taxes on selected products.

DEFICIT BONDS

Faced with implacable resistance to increases in personal income taxes, and a flattened curve of revenue from the economy, the Japanese were forced to turn to deficit bonds to make up the deficit, and since 1974, a growing percentage of the budget has been financed in this manner.

The amount of such outstanding debt has risen from about 10% of the Gross National Product (GNP) in 1975 to just over 36% in 1982. The long-term debt as a percent of GNP now stands at 47.7%, compared to 27.5% in the United States (1980 figure, now much higher), and 15.1% in West Germany (1980).

The Trust Fund Bureau is the part of the Ministry of Finance which handles all funds which are paid into the treasury and earmarked for specific purposes. More and more, this Trust Fund Bureau has become the underwriter of these deficit bonds, and private financial institutions have been getting out from under this less profitable burden of buying the government's bonds. But the trust funds which the Bureau administers are therefore being increasingly diverted from their ostensible purposes to underwrite deficit bonds. This means that there are fewer funds available for public works like highway construction, flood control, and airport construction. A comparable situation in the United States might be if gas taxes paid by airlines, and ticket taxes paid by airline passengers were diverted from the trust fund for operation of the air traffic control system and the financing of airport development, and used instead to pay for part of the general national budgetary deficit financing.

Thus, the careful arrangements of the Japanese tax system scaled to a deficit-free level of government expenditure has, for more than a decade, been distorted by an unwillingness of the political system to raise taxes, and the inability to retrench government expenditure. It is an all too familiar pattern, and the use of deficit bonds is widely deplored by economists, public administrators, businessmen, and the general public. And even further pressure must now be expected. Deficit bonds have been issued for ten-year terms. They cannot be legally refinanced and must be paid in full at expiration. Those 5.3 billion yen of bonds first issued in 1975 became due in 1985, and the Ministry of Finance was forced to budget funds for their redemption. But this leaves more than 135 billion yen in bonds due in increasingly large amounts for each new fiscal year. The Japanese government faces the alternatives of further retirements out of current income, issuing new deficit bonds to finance the old ones, or changing the law to permit the old bonds to be re-funded. The Provisional Commission for Administrative Reform has urgently recommended in its 1984 final report that "in issuing bonds in the future, the total outstanding should be steadily reduced to bring an end to the dependencies on deficit covering bonds", and it also noted that "resorting to such tentative measures to make ends meet will only keep the real solutions from being executed".[2]

Notes

1.   Drucker, Peter F., "Economic Realities and Enterprise Strategy", *Modern Japanese Organization and Decision-Making*, pp. 228–36, Berkley, California: University of California Press.
2.   "The Final Report of the Provisional Commission on Administrative Reform", p. 127.

4 The Exercise of Central Government Authority: the Budget

Those who deal with and understand the public budget system in United States government will see much that seems the same in the Japanese system. In both cases, it is useful to think about the budget in phases — the managerial phase and the political phase — although of course they meld together. The great surprise which emerges for American observers is the relative value of these two phases in terms of how the **substance** of the budget is really determined.

In the US Federal Government, the last 20–30 years have witnessed the distinct decline of what might be called the professional manager's budget. In theory, Congress enacts general enabling legislation which defines public programs and sets a general framework within which the departments and agencies of the executive branch define actual program needs and compute estimates of the funds needed to achieve them. Congress theoretically reviews these proposals to determine whether they properly implement the intent of the law, make program and fiscal sense, and can be afforded within total budget demand.

The reality, however, has departed very substantially from this theory. For an extended period of 30 years or more, the Congress has extended its reach into more and more detailed levels of agency program policy and operations. The number of "line items" in each congressional budget enactment has grown. Enabling statutes which define programs have become increasingly detailed and explicit, locking in statute more and more of the second- and third-level policies or processes which previously had been left to the judgement and discretion of each agency's apppointed political leadership or its professional career executives and managers.

This trend has produced a highly "political" budget; that is, more and more of the specifics of the executive branch budget have been dictated by the political views of the Congress (and the White House), and less and less is being left to the exercise of judgement by the professional managers in government. This conversion has been proceeding at the same time as the much more visible and important shift in the nature of the budget from an allocation of wealth to an allocation of scarcity. As the budget has become more and more a political battle-ground for highly sensitive and conflict-ridden decisions about the allocation of scarce resources, the value of the budget as a stable basis for program planning has markedly deteriorated, because management plans simply lose all reality until the political maneuvering, negotiation, and compromise are completed. Since this is seldom if ever completed prior to the beginning of the fiscal year for which management plans were prepared, these plans must be discarded and replaced by hastily revamped operating procedures to carry out what emerged from the political decision-making process. In short, the value of planning in a management sense has been largely dissipated except for the most stable and least controversial programs.

These more stringent and more detailed statutory interventions inevitably carry over into the other forms of congressional oversight and control. More detailed authorizing and appropriations legislation means that even operational procedures of the agencies must be carried out in conformance with these details. Then agencies are held accountable for such details by the Congress, or in fact to a small piece of the Congress in the form of one or more sub-committees in each House which have jurisdiction. It also means that the Congress itself is obliged to spend more and more of its own limited time on these modest matters.

The power base of the departments and agencies is further eroded because constituents and client groups find it less and less productive to deal with these agencies, knowing the degree to which both policy and process have been locked into statute, and knowing also that ultimate authority to decide even small details rests with the political leadership. Over time, therefore, the formulation of agency budgets has declined as a management system.

With this as a comparative background, let us now look at the preparation of the Japanese national government budget.

BUDGET FORMULATION

A far higher proportion of the substance of the national budget over the last 30 years represents the results of the planning and program definition of the professional staff of the ministries, as opposed to the political negotiations which dictate substance in the US. It is considered absolutely extraordinary for the Japanese Diet to attempt to change any of the basic policy decisions which undergird the budget, or the plans which the budget is called upon to finance. There is simply nothing between the Diet and the executive branch which begins to approach the level of detailed intervention which characterizes the United States Congress. This does not mean that Japanese political leadership does not have the means to influence the substance of the budget, but it does mean that the Diet as an institution is largely irrelevant, and the political leadership must bring its influence to bear in other ways.

The strongest vehicle for political leadership is the Cabinet, and it attempts to begin the exercise of its influence over the ministries through the initial establishment of the groundrules or "standards" which were issued to the ministries as guides for the preparation of their initial budget estimates.

The official fiscal year runs from April 1 to March 31, and the opening stages of each annual budget formulation cycle begins about the middle of July when the Cabinet supposedly prepares its basic policy guidance to be issued by the Ministry of Finance to the ministries. There are several elements of the offices of the Cabinet and of the Prime Minister which are designed to assist in the formulation of this guidance. Of basic importance is the Ministry of Finance itself which computes the likely revenues of the government and supplies to the Cabinet (and the Liberal Democratic Party) the estimates on which to base budget planning.

Of considerable importance is the Economic Planning Agency which "tracks" the economy and supplies useful insights on economic trends, soft areas, and likely threats and opportunities. In addition, it prepares the formal economic assumptions which are generally accepted as the basis for budget planning throughout the government.

The Tax Commission which is another advisory body in the office of the Prime Minister prepares analyses and recommendations to the Cabinet on tax policy issues, including recommendations for changes in tax policy which could enhance the revenue stream. In addition, there is the Fiscal System Council and the Government Bond Issue Advisory Group which advise the Minister of Finance about the demands for issuance of further government bonds, the needs for budget provisions for debt service, or changes in the fiscal structure and process.

All of these organizations represent resources available to the Prime Minister and the Cabinet, and they often serve as the means to refute, or at least argue with the cases presented to the Prime Minister from the all-powerful ministries. These advisory bodies also freely communicate with the political policy formulation apparatus of the LDP and represent an important way for the party to influence the Cabinet's initial "standards" which set the guidance for the ministries.

However, this rational structure for formulation of political guidance has often proved to be less real than it might be. Often the Cabinet, or perhaps the LDP, is not ready to define its objectives in July, and the Ministry of Finance issues its own version of guidelines to the ministries anyway. Agencies are not necessarily unhappy with this fact, since it means that, in the absence of direction from on high, they are more or less free to advance their own policy views, and let the central political leadership catch up later if they can.

The formulation of the budget within the ministries is certainly not simply a professional, technical matter free from political influence. In fact, many of the really serious political debates take place inside the ministries for two reasons: first, the ministries are very open and sensitive to inputs from the political parties — or at least the LDP — and to the views of client groups and local governments. These views may either come direct, or indirectly through party lobbyists or Dietmen who play a direct role in lobbying the ministries for constituent interests.

Second, much of the political debate is conducted by factions within the ministries themselves. There is no clear line of demarcation in the bureaucracy between "careerists" and politicians. Many younger officials are both — they are people who are essentially politicians but who pursue their careers by a progression of increasingly important posts in one or more ministries. The more successful of these can rise to the top-level political positions up to and including Cabinet Minister and even Prime Minister. Most post-war Prime Ministers have had exactly that kind of experience. These politician/bureaucrats may, at later stages in their careers, be elected to the Diet, or leave government and go to private companies, law firms, or universities where they pursue their political careers from these vantage points.

Thus, many of the best people in the professional staffs of the ministries are political, and there is a constant pattern of internal alliances and networks of people with informal leaders, who debate policies, seeking reinforcement from factions of like-minded people in the party or the Diet; and it is often the results of the maneuvering of these factions which determines policy, even against official Cabinet positions.

At about the end of August, the ministries begin to put the finishing touches to their budget submissions. At that stage, this semi-final product is "cleared" with the Public Affairs Research Council, which is the legislative arm of the LDP, after which the budget is submitted to the Budget Bureau of the Ministry of Finance. In September, October, and November, the Budget Bureau grinds it out with the ministries, enforcing second- and third-level policies of the administration, cutting estimates to conform to previous guidelines where necessary, and highlighting for resolution up the line conflicts which can't be resolved at that level. After the Budget Bureau has done its best, the Minister of Finance convenes a Minister's Budget Conference in early December, out of which comes a document called the "Finance Ministry Draft", and a companion "Budget Compilation Policy" which is a brief general summary of the policies and objectives incorporated in the budget.

It is during this same period of November through early December that the political policy process of the Liberal Democratic Party is most active. The LDP has a set of 18 standing committees which are structured to approximate the responsibilities of the major ministries, and indeed of the standing committees of the Diet. These committees are responsible for policy formulation in their areas, for lobbying the ministries, and for preparation of final negotiation positions for the party leadership. They function under the direction of the Public Affairs Research Council (PARC), which, despite its bland title, exerts perhaps more influence on budget formulation than the national Diet.

PARC prepares its own comprehensive budget position which is reviewed and approved by the Executive Council of the party and transmitted to the Cabinet so that it can be considered prior to the public release of the Finance Ministry Draft.

BUDGET DECISION-MAKING

At this stage, the budget ball game in the Japanese government is largely over. What remains are a few relatively minor accommodations to last-minute ministry or party appeals, and it is particularly interesting how these final decisions are made.

For a period of about a week or ten days, the Cabinet will entertain what are called "revival negotiations". Both Cabinet Ministers and PARC are permitted to place a few "hot" political items on the agenda for a final buy-off session at the official residence of the Prime Minister, at which party officials are present, along with the Minister and Deputy Minister of Finance, the head of the Budget Bureau, and any ministers making appeals. Traditionally, the Ministry of Finance has set aside a special "reserve" fund to pay for any reclamas of this kind. This is **not** an opportunity to propose any serious change in budget policy or estimates. Rather, it is strictly political lubrication, and it is intended to heal wounds, hand out small rewards, grease squeaky wheels, or take care of minor mistakes. But for all that, it represents a valuable technique to forestall any effort to embarrass the whole budget by public fights over small issues.

BUDGET FORMULATION GROUNDRULES

If a large proportion of budget decisions are made by the professional staff of the ministries rather than through political negotiation, how do these decisions get made? There are two kind of answers which are relevant.

First, there is a more or less standard array of techniques and approaches which are applied in any government budget process. These include the following:

1. *Balance/equity*: There is a tendency to avoid conflict by treating every ministry or program about the same. This may involve such things as "across-the-board" or percentage increases or decreases; or increases or decreases in the same percentage as the current budget for each ministry.
2. *Forcing internal priority-setting*: A ministry will be given a deliberately low total funding limitation so that it is forced to allocate scarcity among its own programs.
3. *Distribution formulas*: Funds may be allocated according to computed formulas which are presumed to meet genuine need (i.e. population or population density; average income of citizens; statistical measures such as numbers of school-age children or percentage of elderly, etc.).

4. *Political or external priorities*: Where such policy priorities can be defined, their funding needs will be met in full, and any "short falls" of revenue must be shared more painfully among non-priority programs.
5. *Cost avoidance*: Most budget systems are notorious for deferring the kinds of budget items which can be deferred, such as salary increases, new buildings, maintenance and repair, or entirely new programs ("no new starts").
6. *Performance effectiveness measurements*: Politicians are often loath to consider technical evaluations of program effectiveness for fear that some politically popular programs will be shown to be of little real value, yet this is a necessary and valuable form of managerial budget setting. Where a program can be shown to be obsolete or ineffective (high cost vs. low public value) this is a tool to argue for its reduction or at least for putting it further down on the list of funding priorities.

The second major professional budget formulation technique tends to be planning — real management planning of the kind which is widely used in the private sector world but which is heavily discounted in political systems. There are two excellent examples which are widely used in the Japanese budget system. The first is the recognition of the necessity for "life-of-project" funding for multi-year projects such as highway construction, hardware systems acquisition, or long-term economic development projects. The budget structure makes special provision for considering life-of-project plans for these activities, and once plans are approved, full funding for them is complete and more or less automatic. This avoids the delays and uncertainty created in US government budgeting where such multi-year projects must still go through the roller coaster effects of annual authorization and appropriation.

For the other professional management technique, it is valuable to return to the concept of "scrap and build", which was introduced briefly in the discussion in Chapter 2 about control of government staffing and numbers of organizational entities. The concept of "scrap and build" sounds much like the "zero sum game" so vividly described by Lester Thurow in his book *The Zero Sum Society*[1]. But the Japanese have been using this as a management and budget technique starting after World War II, and with greatest effect since the beginning of the serious budget constraints of 1965 to the present.

Under this concept, if more staff, or a new program, or a new organization must be approved in some arena of government activity, one or more cutbacks elsewhere in government must be achieved to offset the increase. It is not necessarily true that such legitimate cutbacks exist; and yet, for more than 20 years, the imposition of this form of bureaucratic discipline has been a valuable policy, acting as a forcing factor to make such cuts as a condition precedent to acceptance of increases.[2]

But the effectiveness of "scrap and build" has an even deeper impact. Usually, the professional staff of ministries prefer "scrap and build" to arbitrary cuts across the board, because it permits rational planning and decisions, rather than irrational ones. The whole ethic and discipline of the professional manager is designed toward the making of such rational choices on behalf of his institution, and even when such decisions are difficult, the net effect is better and probably more cost-effective management for the public.

Notes

1. Thurow, Lester, *The Zero-Sum Society: Distribution and the Possibilities for Economic Change*, New York: Basic Books, 1980.
2. In a personal letter, Peter Drucker offered the following comment on "scrap and build"; "You allude to the principle that no prefecture or municipality is permitted to engage in a new activity unless its cuts back or sloughs off an old one. This, I am convinced, is the real secret. I admit to being prejudiced. This was my contribution 25 years ago to the Japanese local government policy."

5 The Concepts and Structure of Local Government

Prior to World War II, local governments had little or no independence and were generally treated as administrative arms of the national government. There was no basic constitutional recognition of local governments, and their legal existence rested on a few basic statutes — one for prefectures, one for cities, one for counties (abolished in 1921), and one for towns and villages. Governors of prefectures were local agents of the national government appointed by the Emperor and responsible to him. All local governments were supervised by the powerful Ministry of Home Affairs on most matters, and by other ministries (i.e. Transport, Education, Agriculture) where relevant.

Furthermore, under a complex set of nationally established groundrules, local governments were responsible for sharing the costs of all national government programs, while having little or nothing to say about the politics which defined them, or even the manner of their implementation. Municipalities were fully subordinated to prefectural governors in all but the most minor local issues. The electoral base was very narrow, being primarily male land- or property-owners. Political leadership tended to be an elite of minor nobility and land-owners who viewed themselves not as public servants but as officials of the crown.

The entire period of Japanese development through the 1880s up to World War II was one in which the central government was leading or pushing the country into rapid industrialization. The principal allies forming the government were the military and the rapidly rising class of industrialists, bankers, traders, and small businessmen. The more conservative elements of society were farmers, rural and small town people, and urban workers who were, as in western countries, more often the victims of this economic revolution rather than its beneficiaries. Rural areas, villages and towns, and even the cities tended to be ignored and politically disenfranchised.

But the very process of industrialization began inevitably to force the pace of urbanization. Millions of people left the countryside, which stagnated, and flocked to the cities, which were hard pressed to deal with them. The old style concepts of paternalistic municipal government proved constantly inadequate to meet the burgeoning demands for housing, effective sanitation, health care, transportation, electric power, and the other elements of urban infrastructure needed to support the expanding industrial and commercial base.

This pressure for more and better local governments created two subsidiary tides. First, the pace of growth frustrated the natural urge of the national government to control events while placing as much of the financial responsibility as possible for local services and facilities on the local government. Local governments simply did not have the revenue resources or the powers of taxation to meet these growing needs, and they soon realized that they had to force the national government to pay for its own demands.

The second tide came about as local governments found that, in an increasingly complex economic world, they could successfully argue that the national government could not politically manage everything, and that a greater degree of decentralization of political power was necessary. The demands of an industrial society were being met by a broader base of educated people: a professional class, more skilled craftsmen, and a larger class of small businessmen. These people began to insist on a greater political voice in their own affairs and were capable of exerting more direct influence on the political elite which ran the national government. Universal male suffrage was achieved in 1925 (but not for females until 1947), and the national government, just prior to World War II had already begun to draw back from its total control of local government. But its attitude remained very centralist in nature. This was in part because, even where there was increasing sympathy for strengthening local government, there was no generally accepted theory of how real local autonomy could and should be structured, and how far the power of government could be decentralized without significantly impairing the capacity of the central government.

These trends were intercepted by the Second World War, but they were a powerful influence toward democratization which established a climate for the whole rethinking of Japanese government which followed the end of the war, including a receptivity for the ideas which came from the Allied occupation government.

POST-WAR REDEFINITION OF LOCAL GOVERNMENT

As the Japanese faced the post-war era after World War II, their vision of their own future was positive, assertive, and driven by a recognition that very broad changes were going to be necessary in both private and public institutions. The Meiji Restoration of 1867 represented not only the restoration of the Emperor as unitary head of the State, but a struggle to forge an entirely new government structure capable of directing a modern state. The Japanese government which emerged was highly centralist in character because it was clear that a powerful national government would be required to drive change. In addition, Japanese local government was non-existent, or weak and chaotic — a legacy of the medieval structure of feudal lords which the Meiji Restoration terminated.

From the 1870s until the post-war period, local government went through a protracted period of formation, consolidation, and restructuring; but this was done always under strong controls exercised by the national government under policies which emphasized the dominance of national over local matters, and economic and military expansion over social and personal needs.

But the defeat in World War II created a rejection of these previous concepts, and a watershed in general attitudes about the role of governments. The new Constitution of 1947 emphasized the basic principle of democratic government and fundamental rights, drawing heavily from European and American tradition. It established for the first time the principle of a government of the people, in contrast to a government loyal to the Emperor. Japan committed itself to a structure which carried representative government down to the prefectural level and to cities, towns, and villages. The Constitution itself gave recognition to these bodies equal to that of the national government, and it further stipulated that "Regulations concerning organization and operations of local public entities shall be fixed by law in accordance with the principle of local autonomy" (Article 92). In furtherance of this principle, a Local Autonomy Act was passed which defined a two-tiered structure of prefectures and municipalities of several categories. This act further defined the structure, composition, and powers of local elected legislative bodies, and of chief executives at both levels. While each level is guaranteed by the Constitution and has equal status under it, national policies have continued to be paramount, and the national government retains a superior position. Local by-laws may not violate prefectural by-laws, and prefectural by-laws may not contravene national laws.

This structure of national and local entities is further defined by a series of additional national laws. For example:

1. The Local Public Enterprise Law authorizes the establishment and operation of public enterprises.
2. The Local Public Service Law establishes the present system of civil service employment, along with the Local Public Enterprise Labor Relations Law.
3. The Local Tax Law regulates the tax authorities of local entities.
4. A series of national tax laws defines the basis of payments by the national government. For example, a tax allocation law distributes revenue from the income tax, corporation tax, and liquor tax to local entities by formula. Other laws transfer funds for local roads, airports, and other purposes.
5. Separate laws deal with the establishment and operation of schools, police, and fire protection.
6. The Local Government Finance Law mandates the nature of local government finance and accounting systems and requires certain reviews and approvals at higher government levels.

There are many other statutes which deal with additional aspects of local public administration, but these examples make clear that, while the Japanese people and government were willing to commit themselves to the evolution of substantial autonomy for their newly defined structure of prefectures and municipalities, they would do so in a pattern different from the American experience. Their previous history and tradition of strong central government would not be fully rejected, because their view of the post-war era was that strong central authority would continue to be imperative for economic and social development. But it was recognized that, in order for local governments to become stronger, the central government had to be less dominant. The series of local laws described above all fit into a pattern in which the national government lays down the centrally defined uniform structure and groundrules within which local entities function. This is in substantial contrast with the American tradition of a constitution that dealt only with the national and state governments, and a long history of conflict over the growth of power in the national government that has often meant the impairment of state authority.

The Local Autonomy Law is widely regarded as the document of liberation for Japan's new structure of prefectures and municipalities. Yet by American standards it is a highly centralist instrument. It is true that it sets forth the basic roles and authorities of local governments, and they are extensive. But it goes further by setting forth, often in extreme detail, exactly how these authorities must be exercised.

The system which emerged is very "public administration" oriented in the sense that it contains many elements that also define how the administration or management of public functions is to be carried out. This takes the form of groundrules which lay down administrative policy and standards, but stop just short of imposing such strong central controls that the reality of local autonomy would be frustrated.

Basically, the law says that:

> each local public body shall, in addition to its own community affairs, and the affairs required by national law or by cabinet order, perform other administrative affairs within its area insofar as such affairs are not reserved to the State (i.e. the national government).
>
> (Local Autonomy Law (1947), Article 12)

This is authority conveyed in a form directly opposite to the concept of residual states' rights in the US; that is, specific authorities not given to the national government are reserved to the states. Here the Local Autonomy Law is the instrument by which the national government makes specific designations of roles which it authorizes local governments to exercise.

But the Local Autonomy Law goes far beyond that authorizing role. It becomes the charter which defines the authority of all 47 prefectural assemblies and for all municipal legislative bodies; and it similarly defines the role and limits the powers of governors, mayors, and other public officials. It establishes many uniform rules which must be obeyed, and final approvals which are retained by the national government. A few examples will illustrate the point:

1. The boundaries of local public jurisdictions are defined by national law. Municipal boundaries must be changed by petitioning the Minister of Home Affairs, and the incorporation of previously unincorporated areas into existing public bodies can be mandated by the Cabinet.

2. Local governments are empowered to enact by-laws which are not in conflict with national law. Prefectures may enact by-laws which direct the affairs of municipalities. Chief executives may in turn enact regulations which do not conflict with laws or prefectural by-laws.

3. Provision is made for election of assembly members and chief executives, but the full specifics of such elections are set forth in detail in a national election law. The Local Autonomy Law and Cabinet orders specify in detail when and how citizens may: petition for enactment, amendment, or abolition of a by-law; require an audit of public activities; demand the dissolution of the assembly; or demand the removal from office of a public official.

4. With respect to assemblies themselves, the Local Autonomy Law prescribes the numbers of assembly members, when and how the membership is permitted to change, the term of office, the timing of assembly meetings, their powers, how they should conduct their affairs, procedures for demanding testimony or the production of records, enforcement powers, the number and responsibility of its standing committees, and how committees must function.

5. In a similar manner, the powers and authorities of chief executives are defined, including the number, name, and responsibilities of all of the major sub-divisions of the municipal government.

6. The Local Autonomy Law cites innumerable other national laws for the purpose of requiring local government obedience; not just major statutes such as the City Planning Law or the National Environmental Preservation Law, but also the "Law for School Meals for Night Courses of Senior High Schools", or the "Laundry Law" which sets forth detailed procedures for licensing, registration, and examination of laundries and health examinations for their workers.

In total, there are about 550 national laws which define an estimated 70–80% of all of the activities of prefectures and municipalities. There are generic laws which define the basic civil service system for local governments, mandate uniform organizational structures, and establish common administrative procedures. There are laws which require the preparation of local government budgets and funding plans, and mandate their clearance and approval by the Ministry of Home Affairs and the Ministry of Finance at the national level. All plans for the issuance of local bonds must be similarly approved. Local governments are required to prepare general economic development plans and specific plans for transport, environmental protection, housing, education, and almost everything else of consequence; and these plans are all subject to the review and approval of relevant ministries in Tokyo. The Japanese, who favor soft, cooperative sounding phrases refer to the "administrative guidance" of these ministries, when in fact, the network of hard detailed statutes described above, along with a further layer of Cabinet orders and bureaucratic regulations can constitute absolute control whenever the central government finds it necessary.

DELEGATIONS OF NATIONAL AUTHORITY TO GOVERNORS

The national government generally reserves to itself a number of public functions which it performs directly: national law and order, defense, national transportation systems, the judicial structure, communications, the postal service, navigation and waterways, national hospitals and medical facilities, and higher education and training.

There are additional public activities which remain under the control of the central government, but which can be delegated to prefectural governors for implementation. These include: preparation and execution (after approval) of regional development projects: water resources development; alien registration; wildlife protection; environmental preservation; water, air, and noise pollution prevention; mental hygiene hospitals; operations of local social welfare offices; administration of national health insurance; administration of employment security offices; agricultural support programs; registration of automobiles and their safety inspection; operation of harbors, the registration of small vessels and their operation in public waters; and administration of national highways, and the construction of local roads. There are, in all, more than 350 provisions of the Local Autonomy Law which deal with public activities which may be managed by prefectural governments, and a similar list of affairs which can be managed and executed by mayors of cities.

For prefectural governments and municipal mayors, these categorical program relationships are both a blessing and a curse. They are a blessing because, in most cases, they deal with public services vital to the functioning of local governments, and it is better to be responsible for them, even by delegation, than to have them directly performed by the national government.

They are a curse because, once the delegations are accepted, local governments become responsible for the service delivery which the public experiences, and yet, most of the real decisions about funding, priorities, and service levels are shared with, or controlled by the national ministries. Thus, local officials are often in the classic management dilemma of "responsibility without authority", and suffer in the public eye because of it.

In addition it is extremely expensive and time-consuming for local government administrators to do the work necessary to get national government approval of detailed plans, procedures, and operations. These expenses run up the cost of local government, and in tight budget times, such as the last ten years, they can get caught in the "cutback management" pinch. It is undoubtedly infuriating to be a local official dealing with real problems at home while being subjected to "administrative guidance" from several Tokyo ministries to cut costs and improve service delivery.

There is a unique and ominous political threat which accompanies the exercise of these delegated programs. Despite the fact that local government manages these activities using local people and organizations, local elected assemblies have virtually no authority over them. In addition, the relevant minister in the national government can directly order a prefectural governor to carry out certain actions, and if the governor does not obey such orders, he or she can (subject to certain legal appeals) be removed from office by the national minister. Under similar circumstances, a mayor may be removed by a governor for failure to obey orders.

These intergovernmental relationships are enormously complex and probably can't be fully understood by outsiders, but a couple of comparisons with American counterparts is illuminating. In the United States, the messiness of relations between the national government and states, counties, and municipalities makes the Japanese system look like a masterpiece of neatness and simplicity in comparison. Even after the Reagan administration block grants were enacted in 1982–3, there remained approximately 900 grant programs which deploy federally defined programs down through the state/ local governmnet structure. The Japanese system at least has the virtue of dealing directly with governors and mayors, and relying on them to manage public program implementation. In many US situations, public programs can and do bypass these generally elected local officials and convey dollars and program instructions directly to second- and third-level elements of local governments, or to special-purpose political entities. For example, the Administrator of the Urban Mass Transportation Administration could grant funds (sometimes without the approval of the Secretary of Transportation) directly to the general manager of a local transit authority, bypassing both the governor of the state and the chief executives of the local cities and counties in the process.

In Japan, the Local Autonomy Law and other central public administration statutes mandate the general groundrules for administration of public programs, but in the US there may be hundreds of different program-enabling statutes which define utterly different standards, procedures, eligibility requirements, cost-sharing formulas, reporting requirements, and departmental oversight, which makes the job of local public officials intolerable and all but impossible. And this melange of national laws and regulations has been widely criticized as posing the same kind of threat which is built into the Japanese system — that national direction can be so detailed and so intrusive that it can usurp the authority of the local manager and leave him with the job but not the power to satisfy the public need.

GENERAL FINANCIAL RELATIONSHIPS BETWEEN NATIONAL AND LOCAL GOVERNMENTS

Sixty percent of all of the final expenditures of local government are derived from various sources of national government funds. As discussed above, there is a wide range of programs (perhaps 2,100 or more) in which payments are made through the ministries of the national government, either for programs which are delegated to local governments for administration, or for special grants and subsidies for other public purposes. In addition, there are other public programs which are considered shared responsibilities of two or more governmental levels, in which the funding is also shared by some computed formula.

In addition each year the national government distributes a "local allocation tax" by formula. This consists of a statutorily defined percentage (currently 32%) of all revenues collected from the major national taxes — the personal income tax, the corporation tax, and the liquor tax. This fund in its modern form was enacted in 1954 as a means to assure and stabilize the flow of funds to meet "necessary, appropriate, and rationalized" expenses of local governments (Local

Autonomy Law (Article 1). Although the formula presumes that these expenses will be precisely determined by "various coefficients", in fact the sum is politically negotiated and the percentage of tax revenues must be periodically recomputed to remain even approximately realistic.

Finally, there are other special-purpose funds which are confined to specific uses (i.e. gas taxes for road construction) which are collected on behalf of local governments as an administrative convenience, and simply transferred to them on collection.

These national funds are supplemented by local government tax revenues and the issuance of local bonds which will be discussed in more detail in the next chapter.

There is no arena of intergovernmental relations which is the subject of more conflict than this one. Local governments must measure the public demands for both local community programs and those programs which it administers jointly with, or on behalf of, the national government and they must put these budget estimates into the budget cycle of the national government. Especially during the last few years since 1975, when the national government has operated at growing deficits, local governments have felt that they have not received a realistic share of total public revenue. They believe that both political and bureaucratic pressures in Tokyo have not kept the stream of funding up with inflation; that public programs have not kept pace with rapid urbanization and industrial infrastrucure demands; and with rapidly evolving changes in social expectations, especially in housing and environmental preservation. The national government in turn points urgently to the flattened curve of national economic growth; the cumulative consequences of 20 years of meeting new social expectations; and the general feeling that local governments need to trim their fat and rein in their own public service commitments.

THE FUTURE OF LOCAL AUTONOMY

From the vantage point of the distant outside observer, the achievements of local autonomy seem extraordinary and magnificent. Starting from a very low base in a war-ravaged nation, in the short period of 40 years, the Japanese have created an entirely new structure of local governments which have proved to be highly democratic in character and have generally stood up well to the demands of an exceptional period of rapid urbanization and sophisticated economic development. Japan now closely approximates the degree of social development found in other industrial nations, and its population has enjoyed a generally equitable sharing of wealth and improvement in the standard of living which its powerful economic system has generated. Japanese cities are densely populated and very industrial, but they appear clean and well run. Japanese culture has proved fascinating in its ability to absorb foreign influence and select what it wants from it while still preserving the best of its own highly valued cultural heritage.

Within Japanese society, however, the success of the local autonomy movement is still the subject of much critical debate and uncertainty. But this is not a debate about failure. There is a broad underlying debate about how well and how swiftly the fundamental conception of strong independent local government, as envisioned in the Constitution, is being realized; and in recent years there has grown up a more urgent and short-term debate about the new strains and constraints placed on the evolution of local autonomy by the era of deficit public finance.

There are notable comparisons which can be drawn between the broad tides of Japanese public administration and those in the United States. The Kennedy and Johnson years in the US were a period of high expectations, when it was thought that the US economy could finance the solution to every kind of public problem, and that there could be a superior kind of understanding in Washington which could find those solutions. There was perhaps an over-eager willingness to accept the concepts of Keynesian economics which justified public deficit financing because it was thought to stimulate the economy so that it could support higher levels of taxation. And then there was a broad tide of public disappointment and disenchantment with the inability of the federal government to solve all problems, and a growing fear of big government and intractable deficits.

During the period of 1950 to about 1965 the Japanese too began to believe that their economic miracle was endless, and there was a great tide of new public programs, most of them fully justified. The decision in 1975 to begin to issue bonds for deficit financing was also justified in Keynesian terms. But as the economy began to level off, and as the Japanese government observed the trends in the US and elsewhere, they too began to reconsider more seriously what government they could afford, and to draw back from the euphoria induced by their economic growth.

It is therefore not coincidental that there are such similarities between the presidency of Ronald Regan and the policies of the Nakasone administration. And just as Nixon, Ford, and even Carter set the stage for Reagan, Prime Ministers before Nakasone set the stage for this major rethinking of the roles and capabilities of government which has been a hallmark of the Nakasone period. Both countries have instituted major programs of administrative reform, constraint of governmental expenditures, reductions in public workforces, and exploration of ways to "privatize" public functions. Both have placed great emphasis on the need to use the resources and leverage of governments to revitalize economic growth before committing themselves to further growth in the deficit-ridden public sector.

Within these broad tides, the debate about local autonomy becomes more understandable. One school of thought argues that the highly centralized and controlled national government presence in local government affairs described in this chapter is not changing fast enough, and that the very structure of government, and the political and bureaucratic inertia of it simply will not permit a faster pace of local political independence. In this view, the leveling of the economy and the fears surrounding high-deficit public budgets will strengthen the hand of the centralists and slow the pace of the local autonomy movement.

The other view seems to be that things are changing and that fears about the economy and deficits will expedite the pace of change rather than stultify it. There are some current trends which give support to this view. Over the past few years, the Ministry of Finance has supported the concept that a higher proportion of public revenue should be locally generated, and while the Finance Ministry argues for its own benefit, this view has lent strength to prefectural and municipal governments who are willing to accept this financial burden if accompanied by greater political authority. Local government expenditure has increased, both as a percentage of gross national product and as a percentage of total government expenditure.

The recommendations of the Nakasone Provisional Commission for Administrative Reform also strongly emphasize the values of further decentralization of both political and administrative authority to local governments, somewhat cynically as a means to shift taxing burdens, but also as a genuine policy preference for future good government.

6 The Basic Structure and Authorities of Local Governments

The Japanese have an affinity for neat, clean, and relatively disciplined structures of government, and the nature of their 1947 Constitution has permitted them to carry that discipline into the design of local governments. The basic structure and authorities of prefectures and municipalities have been defined not by those governments themselves, but by a series of national laws which mandate essentially the same institutional architecture at all three levels. A look at prefectures will illustrate the point.

PREFECTURES AND MUNICIPALITIES

There are 47 prefectures; 43 which are equivalent to US states, and three cities (Tokyo, Osaka, and Kyoto) and one district (Hokkaido) which have been given special authorities equivalent to a prefecture. Each has a bi-cameral legislative body called an Assembly, and as in the national Diet, the lower House is by far the stronger. Assembly members are elected for four-year terms, and the membership ranges from twelve to 130 depending on total population. The governor convenes the Assembly four times a year and may call special sessions when needed, and he may dissolve the Assembly and call for elections. Most votes are by simple majority, but certain important actions may require a two-thirds vote.

While the role of prefectures are broad-ranging, the Local Autonomy Act, which defines their authorities, does not define a fully independent body capable of doing anything. Rather, it defines a more limited purpose for prefectures as a coordinative layer of government primarily to direct activities which require uniformity in performance, cover a wide geographical area, are deemed too extensive for management by municipalities, or require efforts to coordinate two or more cities, towns, or villages. In general, all activities of the prefecture are under the direct authority of the Governor as chief executive. His powers include the right to submit legislation to the Assembly, to prepare and execute budgets, to levy and collect local taxes, fees, and charges. He appoints and supervises all public employees, and organizes and manages the departments of the government, including ownership and management of all public facilities. He may also let contracts, or establish and supervise public enterprises to carry out the public's business. All elements of the government report to him except that there is an independent Public Safety Commission to supervise the police force, and an Education Commission appointed by him but with the consent of the Assembly which administers all school systems and other educational, cultural, and scientific facilities.

There is also an independent Election Commission appointed by the Assembly, and an Audit and Inspection Commission, a Treasurer, and Chief Accountant, all of whom are appointed by the Governor, but operate independently and cannot be removed by him.

Governors submit a high proportion of new legislation each year, and have veto powers on bills. The Assembly may override vetos, with two-thirds of the votes required in many cases. The Assembly may pass a "resolution of non-confidence" by vote of two-thirds of the membership. Chief executives in turn can dissolve the Assembly, but in that case the Asembly, after reconvening, may oust the Governor by a simple majority vote of non-confidence. Municipal governments have an almost exactly similar structure as Assemblies, and mayors as chief executives have similar powers and duties.

What do local governments actually do?

In fact, they are the major deliverers of public services. Within the framework and structures and authorities described above, local governments have a very broad range of public programs which they manage. These can be grouped as follows:

1. *Public law and order*: local courts, police, law enforcement rules and regulations.
2. *Health and welfare*: hospitals, welfare facilities, nurseries, sanitoria, correctional facilities, burial facilities, environmental protection.
3. *Infrastructure*: roads, bridges, canals, waterways, transport, docks, piers and wharves; land development and reclamation; industrial development; agricultural assistance; water and sewer facilities; gas and electrical power; parks and playgrounds.
4. *Education and culture*: schools, laboratories, and experimental

facilities; libraries, museums, art galleries, theaters, gymnasiums and public halls; historic preservation and scenic beauty.

For each of these public programs the authority of the Governor includes planning, construction and maintenance of facilities, regulation and zoning, management, inspection and compliance, and the maintenance of necessary records, registrations, reports, and statistics.

It needs to be emphasized again that Prefectural Governors are in a particularly complicated and difficult position in the conduct of these programs because of the involvement of the national ministries in almost every one of these arenas. In addition to budget and financial controls (see next chapter) there are numerous bureaucratic authorities which the national government retains. These include the right to demand a big selection of reports and evaluations of performance; the right to conduct investigations, inspections, and audits of local government activities; and the right to impose "measures for correction" for inadequate performance or violation of national laws, regulations, and Cabinet orders.

THE COMPARATIVE "EFFICIENCY" OF PUBLIC STRUCTURE

This book is full of references to the fact that the Japanese themselves are constantly worried about the size of their governmental establishment, and are constantly seeking ways to cut back the size and cost of the civil service staff. Yet the relatively clean and sparse institutional structure described here employs far fewer public employees per one thousand citizens than other major countries. Table 6.1 shows this comparison for Japan and the United States.

Table 6.1:   Comparison: Number of Public Employees
(in millions)

	Japan	US
Total population	117.1('80)	226.5('80)
National government	2.142	4.911
National government (excluding defense)	(1.844)	(1.926)
Local public employees	3.118	13.445
Total	5.260	18.356

Based on these figures, Japan has 44.9 public employees per 1,000 citizens, compared to 82.4 per 1,000 in the United States. These numbers beg the question of how the Japanese in fact appear to manage their public affairs with a substantially smaller workforce in proportion to their population than can the United States. In fact, compared to Japan's 44.9 ratio, numbers in France (82.8), West Germany (75.8), and the United Kingdom (109.4) all look very high.

If there is a real answer to this question it will undoubtedly be very complicated and rest on comparisons which are difficult to make, such as the range of public programs, the extent of each, the extent to which governments have substituted themselves for private sector capabilities, and the resources committed to public regulation and compliance.

One extreme example, which the Japanese figures recognize, is the disparity between the US and Japanese national defense establishment which involves 2.985 million military and civilian personnel in the US and just 298,000 in Japan. Even if these personnel are factored out, however, the ratios are 42.4 to 69.0.

There is one very useful and simple form of assessment which does help to explain these numbers, and that is to break them down by levels of government. Here the discipline of the Japanese structure is apparent. Table 6.2 shows this distribution not only in terms of numbers of employees at each level, but also in terms of the number of government units as well. Then, Table 6.3 shows calculations of the number of public employees per 1,000 citizens for several groupings of governmental units.

There are many inadequacies in these figures. Data is not always from the same year, and there is not full comparability between the constituent elements of these figures.

If suitable caution is exercised in the use of these numbers, they do appear to permit a few conclusions. First, Table 6.3 suggests that the disparity in the relative productivity of the two national governments is not great (18.3 vs. 22.1). If the defense establishments are excluded, and if Japanese public enterprises are also excluded because comparable entities are not recorded in the US numbers, then the resultant figures of 7.7 per 1,000 in Japan and 8.6 per 1,000 in the United States are reasonably close and clearly not part of the overall disparity.

A similar conclusion seems true at the level of US states and Japanese prefectures. Really exact comparisons are particularly

Table 6.2: Comparison: Numbers of Government Units
and their Employment
(in millions)

Type of Government	Japan*		US†	
	# Units	Employees	# Units	Employees
National government	1	2.142	1	4.911
Prefecture/State	47	1.706	50	3.747
Municipal/County				
County	--	----	3,042	1.804
Township	--	----	16,734	.377
Municipality	3,255	1.462	19,076	2.460
School districts	3,278	(1.290)‡	14,851	4.182
Special districts	n/a	n/a	28,588	.502
Sub-total	6,533	1.462	82,291	9.325
Totals	6,581	5.310	82,342	17.983

* "Statistical Abstract of Japanese Local Government", pp. 7,12; Tokyo: Jichi Sogo Center, 1982.

† "1982 Census of Governments, Vol. 1 — Government Organizations"; and "Public Employees in 1982", Bureau of the Census, US Department of Commerce, Washington, DC, 1982.

‡ This number includes prefectural personnel.

distribution of public roles and responsibilities in both countries between the national governments and the state/prefectural level on the one hand, and between these entities and subordinate governments on the other. Nevertheless, if these numbers can be accepted as gross indicators, Table 6.3 suggests that the cost in employee terms of these governments is reasonably comparable.

*Table 6.3:   Comparison: Numbers of Public Employees
per 1,000 Citizens*

	Japan	US
National government	18.3	22.1
National government (excluding national defense)	15.8	8.6
National government (excluding defense and public enterprises)	7.7	8.6
Prefectural/State	14.6	16.5
Municipal etc. (in US: counties, townships, municipalities, school districts, special districts)	12.5	41.2
Municipalities only	12.5	10.9
Counties and townships only	---	9.6
Education only	(11.0)	18.5

It seems clear that the real disparity between US and Japanese public sector employment lies at the sub-state level — 12.5 employees per 1,000 citizens in Japan, vs. 41.2 per 1,000 in the United States. Again, it is extraordinarily hard to draw precise comparisons with respect to the public responsibilities of all these sub-state entities, and the workforces needed to perform them. But Table 6.2 does show one remarkable difference — in the **number** of these sub-state entities. It becomes very hard not to conclude that it is this remarkable difference in the number of government entities which accounts for much of the perceived productivity advantage which the Japanese appear to enjoy.

The intergovernmental architecture which was defined by the new Japanese Constitution was structurally very clean and sparse in comparison to US experience. Japan defines only three government levels — national, prefectural, and municipal. There are no counterparts for 3,049 counties and 16,734 townships found in the US. The Japanese integrate school systems into their prefectural or municipal structure, and while there are more than 3,200 education commissions in Japan to supervise educational programs, this does not really parallel the 14,851 independent school districts in the US which are deliberately outside of regular governments. Finally, while the Japanese use special bodies and public enterprises, these organizations are integrated into municipal structures and have no independent status or taxing powers. Thus, there is no Japanese equivalent of the 28,588 special districts which are reported in the official census of government units.

The United States has 82,342 officially defined and reported units of general and special purpose government compared to Japan's 6,580. This enormous US governmental superstructure is exceedingly costly in terms of the public employment to sustain it. The mere creation of any organization requires at least a minimum of staff simply to open its doors to do business.

The far more complex US pattern of jurisdictions inevitably breeds problems of overlap of authority, duplication of responsibilities, more complicated and expensive communications and coordination, and the high costs of conflict. This is particularly true in a federal system in which there are many federal government or federally funded programs which are deployed down through the state and local governmental structure, including many which link directly with subsidiary organizations in states, counties, and cities and often bypass generally elected officials.

This array of public bodies also varies widely in its relative "productivity" in terms of the people it serves. Seventy-five percent of all counties serve less than 50,000 people, and one Texas county has just 91 residents. More than 9,300 townships serve less than 1,000 citizens, and only 1,019 serve more than 10,000. Ninety-two percent of all special districts have less than two million dollars in debt capability. The number of US sub-state governmental elements has increased modestly between 1967 and 1982 (81,299 to 82,291). Reductions in the number of school districts and townships have been offset by an increase of more than 7,300 special districts, 43% of which have property-taxing powers. But since World War II, the Japanese have capped a long-term trend in the reduction of the number of municipalities by reducing that number from 10,520 in 1945 to the present level of 3,255. Clearly a different philosophy is at work. The proliferation of governmental entities in the US is most frequently justified as highly democratic, since it gives our citizens very localized government supposedly highly responsive to the public will. To the extent that this proliferation is seen as costly and unproductive, it will be argued that this burden is warranted. And yet Japan, too, is a democratic nation. Its governments work at least as well as ours, at far more moderate burden, and the Japanese people appear to accord this system their general approval and support.

7 Local Government Income and Spending

The two most compelling and important tides moving in Japanese society since the war have been the expansion and development of its private sector economic base, and the flowering of its social expectations and institutions leading to a better quality of life for the average citizen. Until a few years ago, these tides were not seen to be in conflict. The Japanese people seem to recognize, more than the citizens of other countries, how closely their new and attractive society is linked to the innovation and vitality of the private sector. The new wealth of the nation has been diffused with reasonable equity across most of the population, and until about ten years ago, it was hard to find fault with the proportion of this national wealth which flowed into governments at all levels. There was wide consensus behind a whole new social agenda. The Japanese are not given to public bragging, but it seems clear that there is a deep-seated belief that Japan can and should be the equal of any nation in the things which characterize a civilized, advanced society: education, culture, health and well-being, modern public infrastructure, and a democratic and responsive government. The Japanese set in simultaneous motion broad public programs to achieve these objectives, financed by the "miracle" economic development.

The watershed for this national course of action came after the oil crisis of the early '70s. While Japan has successfully accommodated to that shock, it seems to have marked the end of that marvelous certainty that economic growth could make all things possible. An important part of that watershed was that, in 1975, for the first time since the war, the Japanese government began to issue "deficit" bonds to finance disparities between government income and expenditures. It appears that at first they felt that such deficit financing would be temporary and that, after a small number of years, economic growth would again generate enough revenue so that desirable new social programs which they had no intention of abandoning could once more be fully sustained. Given the widespread prevalence of this feeling, governments were inclined to retain the patterns of public taxation and expenditure which had evolved over 30 years.

But over the last twelve years, deficit funding has not gone away. Instead, deficits have grown each year, and the perception is also growing that the deficit is somehow built into the economic and governmental system as it is in the United States and most other countries, and that if Japan wants to escape this trap, it must consider sterner and more fundamental changes in order to do so. The need for change seems to have been decided, but how to change the patterns of income and expenditure has become the central issue in local government, and all elements of the fiscal equation are being urgently reconsidered. Income consists of two major streams — the funds taxed by the national government and transferred to the prefectures and municipalities; plus the taxes and fees which local governments are authorized to collect directly. Each of these will be examined in more detail.

LOCAL GOVERNMENT INCOME

The revenue of local governments is usually described in the following six categories:

1. *Local Taxes*: The Constitution and the Local Tax Law authorize local governments to collect a number of taxes that are not in conflict with national tax sources. These are summarized in Tables 7.1 and 7.2.

Table 7.1:   Prefectural Taxes (1982)

Category	% of Total
Prefectural income tax	28.6
Individual	(21.2)
Corporate	(7.4)
Business 'enterprise' taxes	38.1
Individual	(1.3)
Corporate	(36.8)
Real 'property' acquisition	4.0
Tobacco	3.3
Amusement, meal, hotel	6.4
Automobile	10.1
Special 'purpose' taxes	9.1
Auto acquisition	(3.5)
Oil delivery	(5.6)
Other (including discretionary)	.4

Table 7.2:　Municipal Taxes (1982)

Category	% of Total
Municipal income tax	50.4
Individual income	(35.1)
Individual per capita	(.5)
Corporate income	(14.4)
Corporate per capita	(.4)
Fixed assets taxes	32.3
Land	(13.3)
Buildings	(12.1)
Tangible business assets	(5.8)
Other	(1.1)
Motor vehicles	.5
Tobacco consumption	4.7
Electricity	4.1
Gas	.1
Special purpose taxes	7.1
City planning tax	(5.4)
Business office tax	(1.7)
Other (including discretionary)	.8

2. *Local Allocation Tax*: The national government recognized that the capacities of local taxation could not keep up with the demands for local expenditure and thus committed itself to fill this gap, primarily as a means to guarantee the stability of the flow of revenues for all local governments, and in part also to make sure that every local government was assured adequate revenue for its needs. Therefore, by a complex formula, some governments are subsidized through the allocation flow. Under this system, the national government reserves a fixed percentage (currently 32%) of the major taxes it collects from individual and corporate income taxes and the liquor tax and distributes the funds to all local governments. These funds are not earmarked, and local governments may use them as they see fit.
3. *Local Transfer Taxes*: This is similar to general revenue sharing. A statutorily determined amount of national tax revenues are simply distributed to local governments under a formula dealing with the total area of roads. These funds are also not earmarked.
4. *National Government "Specific Purpose" Disbursements*: These funds are made available for two purposes: (1) for national functions delegated to local governments and administered by

them; and (2) total or partial payment for programs solely for national government objectives. Most of these latter funds are obligatory payments to execute programs which are defined by national law, but some are grants in aid which allow some discretion in their use.

5. *Local 'Public' Loans*: The Local Tax Law permits local governments to do some deficit financing in the form of issuance of a bond or certificate redeemable after two or more years, and backed by the full faith and credit of the local government.

6. *Miscellaneous Revenue*: These include fees, service charges, fines and penalties, income from property or investments, and contributions. These income sources are largely within local discretion, and as the fiscal position has tightened, these sources have been more actively explored.

Tables 7.3 and 7.4 summarize the proportion of local revenues obtained from each of these sources.

Table 7.3:   Sources of Revenue: Prefectures (1982)

Items	Percent
Local taxes	33.2
Local allocation taxes	17.9
Local transfer taxes	.7
National government disbursements	25.6
Local public loans	8.5
Miscellaneous revenue	11.2
All other	2.9

Table 7.4:   Sources of Revenue: Municipalities (1982)

Items	Percent
Local taxes	34.7
Local allocation taxes	15.5
Local transfer taxes	1.0
National government disbursements	14.6
Local public loans	9.9
Prefectural transfers	5.8
Miscellaneous	5.9
All other	12.6

Looking further at the sources of local taxes for prefectures, the Local Tax Law defines which local taxes may be collected, but prefectural by-laws spell out specific taxable items, tax objectives, and tax bases and rates. The most important are these:

1. Prefectural income taxes (called the "inhabitant" tax). The individual income tax has two components: a tax based on income with certain deductions and allowances as in the American system; and a "per capita" tax which is essentially a fee for residency. Corporate income taxes have the same two components, but the per capita portion is based on the number of employees and the fixed capital of the corporation. The tax base for both is very similar to that established for the national tax system.
2. The enterprise tax is assessed against both corporations and unincorporated businesses, and is based on net income. For individuals, this is a flat rate of from 3% to 5%. For larger corporations, there is a progressive scale ranging between 6% and 12%.

The enterprise tax is the largest source of income, producing 38.1% of total revenues (1982), mostly from larger corporations. Individual income taxes produce about 21% and corporate income about 7.5%. Automobile taxes of various kinds represent another 13.5%, and hotel taxes and fuel delivery taxes about 5% each.

In cities, the individual income tax produces 50.4% of all revenue. Corporate taxes are worth about 15%, and taxes on land, buildings, and other assets bring in about 32.3%.

Over the years, there have been significant shifts in these patterns of local taxation. In 1960, prefectures got only 6% of their revenues from individual income taxes, and now they get more than 21%. The trade-off seems to have been primarily a reduction in corporate enterprise taxes which were 50% in 1960 and are now below 37%. Another shift of significance is in automobile taxes which, understandably, have climbed from 4% to 13.5%.

In municipalities, a shift of similar magnitude has occurred. Individual income taxes have gone from 33% to 50.4%, while fixed asset (property) taxes declined from 43% to just over 32%.

INTERPRETATION OF THE REVENUE EQUATION

It is perhaps less important to try to understand the dynamics which affect each of these tax categories than it is to understand the general public's attitudes about their taxes and how these attitudes effect the local revenue equation. As described above, the three major sources of local government revenue are transfers from the national government, taxes on individuals, and taxes on corporations. As discussed in Chapter 3, what has emerged over the last decade or more is a total resistance on the part of the whole of the Japanese public against further personal tax increases. This resistance is so implacable that it is seen as political suicide to confront it; and thus it is all but impossible to deal with the current tide of deficit government financing by any significant increases in these taxes. Japanese local government may be able to maneuver at the margin with the per capita tax, or tobacco taxes, or user charges for public services, but these are not large revenue producers. Even increases in these taxes infuriate the public not because they are necessarily onerous in themselves, but because they are seen as coming **on top of** income taxes which are deemed barely tolerable.

To some degree, corporate taxes have been a safety valve in recent years, but there appears to be a real fear that throwing a much greater burden on corporations might threaten economic growth. Nobody really knows where the point of economic stultification might be, but the fear is a serious modulating force against the urge to impose further corporate taxation.

The main political argument now for local government centers around transfers of funds from the national government. There are legitimate concerns about why these funds cannot be increased. The national government itself has operated on deficit financing for eleven years and obviously the flattened growth pattern of the economy has hit national revenues harder than local governments, some of which are actually in a stronger financial position than the national government. In addition, the lower level of economic growth has precipitated a strong national government fiscal reform program to **cut** government costs rather than increase them. This translates into stiff opposition toward any ideas for deploying more funds to local governments.

But one avenue of revenue enhancement for local governments is still being kept open. As part of the broad tide of movement toward local autonomy, there are many leaders in local communities —

politicians, officials, academics, businessmen — who are pressing for a trade-off under which local governments might accept a greater share of the total tax burden if it is accompanied by really significant increases in local autonomy. These ideas generally advocate that certain programs be effectively transferred from the policy control and direction of the national government to local governments. But this transfer has to be accompanied by changes in the whole national tax system which would reduce national taxes by an appropriate degree and permit the increase of local taxes in like amounts. This is a "zero sum" game in terms of the total of taxes currently collected, but it has gained significant backing at the national level. The Nakasone Provisional Commission on Administrative Reform supports this general concept both as a means to relieve the pressure on the national budget, and as a genuine step forward toward the goal of local autonomy. The Ministry of Finance has guardedly supported the concept, not so much for present concerns, but in the belief that future increases in the costs of transferred programs would be absorbed by local governments and not by the national treasury.

LOCAL GOVERNMENT SPENDING

In the previous discussion, it was pointed out that the problems of local finance are mounting, but that the Japanese are locked into patterns of taxation and transfers of funds which are highly inflexible both politically and bureaucratically, primarily because of implacable public resistance to personal tax increases.

Unfortunately, there are comparable unyielding public attitudes which guard the advances in public programs achieved in the last 40 years, and these attitudes seriously constrain the ability of politicians and the career bureaucracy from making changes in the program base and the patterns and amounts of government spending. There is nothing new or different about the Japanese experience. They are suffering the same lessons being brought home to roost in governments all over the world: the political system finds it very easy and politically profitable to initiate or expand public programs, but almost impossible to abandon or retrench them once they are embedded in society and in the lives of people. It is as if the great machine of government can run only in the direction of "more" and it has no reverse gear, or even brakes good enough to slow it down.

When economic growth leveled off in the '70s, the revenue from local taxes leveled off as well, and in turn forced a leveling of fund transfers to local governments. When the national government made fateful decisions in 1975–6 to start deficit bond financing, and an enhanced program of public works construction as an economic stimulation, local governments had little option but to also adopt these "solutions". The last twelve years have left all governments with a legacy of major deficits, greater costs of debt service, and much-reduced fiscal flexibility and room to maneuver. In addition, as governments have attempted to shift to a policy of "restoration of fiscal balance without increased taxation", they have triggered the defense mechanisms of client groups and constituent interests as never before.

THE LOCAL GOVERNMENT PUBLIC FINANCE PROGRAM

The bulk of public employees are at local government levels, which deliver most public services, but real control of these services is in Tokyo. This control is evident in the patterns of funding, but is primarily exercised through the thousands of pages of statutes, Cabinet orders, ministerial regulations, and "administrative guidance" which define these activities in detail.

The national government receives about 63% of all taxes, but when it comes to expenditures, local governments spend more than 73% of all revenues. The national tax machinery thus supplies about 40% of the estimated 55 billion yen which local governments spend each year. The whole complex set of financial relationships is captured in detail in what is known as the Local Public Finance Program which is a national government product. It is assembled and defended by the Ministry of Home Affairs, but the real power resides in the Ministry of Finance and the Cabinet. This is far more than just a summary of funds to be transferred. Each year, the national government makes an official estimate of the revenues and expenditures of local governments. This estimate is combined with the array of national government policies for each program to produce an "acceptable" income-expenditure plan. This plan is really a budget and it is subject to all of the ills and unrealities common to all budget processes. But when the plan is approved by the Cabinet, it locks up local governments in terms of their own local taxes, their local loan programs, their employment and general administrative expenses, and most importantly, the levels of funding for almost all public programs.

Table 7.5 shows the distribution of funds by program area, arrayed in descending order of local government spending. Finally, Table 7.6 takes those major purposes and shows the somewhat different patterns of spending between prefectures and municipalities.

Table 7.5: Government Expenditure by Area (1982)

Program Area	% of total	% by local government
Public health	4.2	92
Education	17.6	87
Land conservation and development	18.8	78
Judicial and police	4.3	78
Housing	2.3	73
Commerce and industry	3.7	68
Miscellaneous (all other programs)	11.9	58
Social welfare	15.0	50
Debt service	14.0	39
Agriculture, forestry, and fisheries	5.0	34
Defense	3.2	--

Table 7.6: Local Spending by Purpose (1982)

Purpose	% by prefectures	% by municipalities
Education	28.8	17.6
Miscellaneous (all other programs)	25.7	18.5
Public works	18.8	20.1
Social welfare and security	5.8	17.2
Agriculture, fisheries	11.0	6.3
Health and sanitation	4.1	7.9
Other	5.8	12.4

8 Policy, Regulation, and Administrative Guidance

It must seem strange to American readers who are so used to the ascendency of the politician to learn about a government in which the center of gravity for public policy formulation lies in the hands of the professional staffs of government agencies rather than in the legislative body. It is interesting to speculate whether the role of the professional public administrator would be as strong if Japan had not had a single ruling political party for so many years, and if one or more of the other political parties had succeeded in creating viable political agendas in competition with the Liberal Democratic Party. Had that happened, it seems likely that more of the debate, negotiation, and policy decision-making would have taken place outside of the ministries in the Diet or in public forums. Had there been other parties coming into office, it seems likely that the political differences inside the ministries would have shifted and changed much more than they have. While the internal conflicts between factions in or between ministries has been fierce, and has been a force for the consideration of alternative policies, it certainly has not produced any substantial departures from the broad national policy mainstreams laid down by the LDP and successive LDP-dominated Diets and Cabinets.

While the Diet is "weak" in comparison with the US Congress, it has still managed to play a respectable role in overall national policy formulation, and has occasionally risen to the need when major new policies are warranted. For example, when, in the 1960s, the Japanese began to realize what was happening to their environment because of the rapid expansion of heavy industry, the Diet swiftly passed a series of anti-pollution laws which, in many respects, are tougher than those in the United States and other nations. During 1967, a Pollution Countermeasures Basic Law was passed which set standards for prevention or reduction of pollution not only of air and water, but of noise, vibration, offensive odors, land subsidence, and agricultural practices. By 1970, these basic standards had been amplified by 14 additional more specific anti-pollution laws relating to specific source problems. These laws also made it clear that enforcement would be carried out even where it might have adverse consequences on the long-term government imperatives for economic development.

These laws were the result of a very substantial surge of general public opinion — perhaps the first — and one of the finest instances of the general public forcing the hand of the government from outside of the normal rings of power. Many of these anti-pollution measures were strongly opposed by the MITI, which failed to recognize or consider the environmental damage stemming from its 20 years of high speed industrial development policy. It should be noted, however, that "A decade later, MITI was to be credited with carrying out one of the most effective industrial cleanup campaigns in history, and in the process, it also developed a thriving new industry in antipollution devices."[1]

There is an excellent case to be made for the effectiveness of the policy formulation process which the career professionals have led, despite the trepidations of the advocates of the political decision-making model. Put another way, Japanese government planners and managers haven't done badly, and lots of politicians have done worse. The Japanese government has successfully faced an enormous array of economic and social problems over the last 40 years, and in general, it has generated appropriate new policies and carried them through into implementation swiftly and effectively.

NATIONAL ECONOMIC DEVELOPMENT POLICY

During the post-war period, these policies were centered around commitments to **high speed** industrial growth which involved concentration on the creation or revitalization of heavy industry such as steel, shipbuilding, electrical power, nuclear power, coal production, the build-up of production of machine tool and heavy electrical equipment industries, and especially, automobiles. But what is so important, and so characteristic of the Japanese government — in disturbing contrast to the American government — is that these policies were understood to drive or frustrate many other elements of economic and social development. It was therefore further understood that they could not be effectively and intelligently pursued unless they were made a part of a comprehensive planning process which guided the whole nation. Planning is a **management** process, and it is one of the primary skills of the professional manager or public administrator rather than the politician. The generation of a broad, comprehensive series of government plans, and the effective implementation of those plans for the whole nation through the instrumentalities of government is perhaps the finest achievement of Japanese public administration.

This seems especially true because, given the breadth, magnitude, and swiftness which were required to resurrect post-war Japan and put it on a successful path of national development, only the government could have provided this leadership. It is useless to suggest that a more political and less managerial system could have done as well or better. The problem rested in the hands of the professional public managers and they performed in an extraordinary manner.

Part of the consequences of high speed industrial development was that it radically changed national demographics, resulting in such rapid movement of rural and small town people to the cities that inadequate urban infrastructures could easily have been totally overwhelmed. But the national ministries were sufficiently coherent in their plans that they were able to help strengthen the financial resources and stability of local governments to cope with this surge. Special plans emerged not only to build up the urban infrastructure of streets, water sources, sewerage disposal, power supply, and transportation, but reasonably well related plans addressed the needs for new housing, more schools, more hospitals and special clinics for the population of people who were becoming the new industrial workforce. For example, if a new industrial park was established in order to locate new companies, a special Industrial Development Plan was initiated by the relevant national ministries which dealt with industrial access roads, power and water demands, rail access, port facilities, and new housing and schools. These plans included, by law, the participation and discussion of the local governments in the formulation of the plans, and a large degree of local government control over the execution of the plans, and the regulation of industries in compliance with them and with local government by-laws and administrative controls.

Another element of these high speed industrial development policies was the collateral decisions to shift away from some traditional older Japanese industries such as textiles, paper products, forestry and agriculture. But development plans also included a pattern of assistance to protect these industries, or mitigate the adverse impacts on them. Where necessary, some low priority industries, or those which did not fit into the export-oriented priorities of economic policy were deliberately phased down, and both capital and labor were shifted to higher priorities.

While high speed industrial development was the central driving policy of the '50s and '60s, national plans were also vigorously pursued to expand and upgrade the educational system, and to expand medical facilities and create a whole new system of medical insurance, social welfare programs, income security programs, and retirement protection. These simultaneous needs created tremendous growth in the financial demands of the public sector which eventually led to deficit financing, but it appears that at least these social policies and plans were reasonably integrated with economic growth through comprehensive planning so that conflict and wastage were kept surprisingly moderate, given the dramatic changes which were achieved. As Chalmers Johnson put it "The public has been willing to accept the trade-off between bureaucrats occasionally exceeding their mandate and quicker and more effective economic administration."[2]

Policy Changes for the '70s and '80s

Praise for the achievements of the Japanese government and private sector does not mean that no mistakes were made or that no problems existed. One of the acid tests of any policy formulation system is whether it is brave enough and flexible enough to meet new needs even when it must therefore abandon old policies of its own creation.

Most of the public problems faced in the '70s were internal to the Japanese economy and society and not forced on it by external events, with two notable exceptions: the energy crisis created by OPEC and worsening economic relations with the US starting with the Nixon and Kennedy years. High speed industrial development had so concentrated capital investment in the private sector that it had led to neglect of non-priority industry and small business. In addition, it was widely argued that, despite the pattern of public funds flowing to local governments, there had still been inadequate investment in local public facilities other than the infrastructure directly needed by industry. There was also the serious problem that many areas of the country had been all but denuded of population to feed the growth of the large industrial cities. The rapid increase in industrial pollution has already been mentioned.

During the '70s and '80s, significant shifts in economic policy were undertaken, based on the following general policies:

1. A slow and often reluctant shift away from the previous patterns of export-oriented industrial development and protection of the home market, toward a pattern of trade liberalization or "internationalism", which loosened up controls and permitted somewhat greater opportunities for foreign sales and foreign investment in Japan.
2. A collateral shift in attention away from heavy industry to product lines which still have a high value-added content, but which rely more on new "high technology". This also includes more attention to the growth of the service sectors of business, and the deliberate enlargement of consumer goods enterprises (so that the "three sacred treasures" of the '60s — television, washing machine, and refrigerator — could be joined by the "three Cs" of the '70s — car, cooler, and color TV). Part of this new policy is the emphasis on further improvements in industrial efficiency through the development and introduction of computer-driven robotic manufacturing techniques. One of the hopes or expectations of this new "high tech." emphasis is that it will permit reduction of high polluting heavy industry, and also a second wave of planned industrial development which will place some of these new operations in underdeveloped areas to redistribute the workforce and relieve some of the overcrowding which has been an element of the old policies.

One of the consequences of this shift has been a growing feeling that the government cannot, in the future, continue to exercise the degree of detailed vertical control over all elements of each priority industry which has characterized the policy of MITI and other ministries in the past. Micro-level control by government, which thinks it can orchestrate all the details, is probably fading. But it is not likely that this signals any serious abandonment of the basic concept of comprehensive national economic policy/planning direction, or the total or even partial abandonment of the marvelous skills of "administrative guidance".

ADMINISTRATIVE GUIDANCE

A little later we will discuss the regulatory powers of Japanese governments at all levels, which are authorities defined by law or formal written authorities including the power to enforce compliance.

But between broad policy formulation and detailed administrative regulation, there is a fascinating middle ground involving the exercise of ministerial influence which has become known as "administrative guidance".

Administrative guidance takes as its base of reference and ultimate source of strength and legitimacy the laws, regulations and policy positions, and formal orders of the Cabinet. But it is something more than just strict execution of these formal authorities. It is a varied and ill defined combination of informal techniques by which a ministry carries out its responsibilities and gets what it wants. These techniques include not only regulations and administrative controls but recommendations, suggestions for courses of action, requests, and warnings. Administrative guidance is very often worked out through a variety of committees, councils, working groups, and other bureaucratic devices which permit a ministry to negotiate with its clientele and persuade them to a position or a course of action.

This middle ground of authority usually goes beyond what is enforceable by law or regulation, and enters areas where client groups, interest groups, local governments, or private corporations dealing with the government can say no if they want to. In fact, they most often say yes to some form of action or policy, and therein lies the success of administrative guidance. Why does it work? It is a combination of power and persuasion; of rewards and punishment of leadership and muddling through.

Let's look at an illustration of the kind of administrative guidance which has been used by the Ministry of International Trade and Industry (MITI). MITI is charged with the initiation of economic development programs in the interest of fostering international trade and a stronger economy. In order to put together an economic development program for a given industry, MITI would most likely convene a "policy council" which it would chair and which would include representatives of most of the private companies in that industry. It may also include other interests such as banks, or other ministries of the government. This group in effect becomes a planning and strategy committee for the industry, free of any taint of collusion or anti-trust concern because they have been convened by the government. Such a policy council will be asked to agree with a position advanced by MITI, and if they agree, the position can be swiftly fed into the political policy process and become the policy of the Cabinet.

Enforcement of such a policy position can be achieved by MITI through the formation of one or more "cooperative discussion groups" which are a form of collusion to dictate the terms of operation in the industry. MITI has used such groups to control the patterns of investment in an industry to emphasize national priorities, optimize export potential, cut back in low value product lines, and so forth. These groups can be the vehicles for debating and agreeing to other policy proposals such as industry consolidations or mergers, the allocation of markets, establishment of production limits and the allocation of production quotas to individual companies. Where production cutbacks or export cutbacks are necessary, the bad news is worked out in such "discussion groups". Here also semi-permanent price cartels are formed which fix prices in the industry, and enforce compliance. Finally, these groups may be the forum for agreeing on international trade strategies and tactics for protecting the home market against foreign competition.

Through a network of such councils and working groups, MITI has its hands in the functioning of most of the important industries in Japan, and a network for negotiating out its economic development program. Such a network is justified in the name of effective development and coordination of a comprehensive strategy for the Japanese economy, the success of which is urgently important to all elements of society; and in that sense, administrative guidance is a rational and necessary function of government. But such an approach is also inherently in conflict with both the concept of anti-trust and anti-competitive practices in the private sector, and with the fear that the government is exercising undue influence and domination over a supposedly independent private sector. MITI has, in fact, often been at odds within the bureaucracy with the Fair Trade Commission which is charged with enforcing anti-trust laws and preventing unfair trade practices. The exercise of this high risk form of administrative guidance places MITI in highly sensitive positions, and they have been accused of being in collusion with, and dominated by, "big business"; of being both too lenient and too tough in their relations with foreign corporations; of fostering environmental damage; of creating overcrowded cities, and much else.

A major share of the success of administrative guidance can also be attributed to the fact that ministries are able to deal out an enormously attractive array of rewards for cooperation. If an industry or individual companies are designated as priority elements of an economic development strategy, the government has proved willing to aid them to whatever degree is necessary to enable them to succeed. The tax system permits a wide variety of accommodations, such as rapid amortization of capital assets, special tax exemptions, write-offs of investments for foreign operations, relief from bad debts resulting from export sales, and other techniques. The government has made direct subsidies to finance industrial growth, or it may make preferential loans and loan guarantees to "in" companies. Two of the most successful instruments used by MITI have been the Export–Import Bank which helps finance foreign purchases of Japanese goods, and the Japanese Development Bank (JDB) which puts the enormous potential of government investment funds behind favored companies which are part of the designated strategic industries. The JDB permits the government to supply capital and other funds to industry under subsidy or preferential terms not otherwise available through private lending institutions in order to implement government policy objectives. Who gets what funds is often a part of the process of "administrative guidance".

Other rewards in the arsenal of the government include the granting of loans and loan guarantees, often at subsidy rates, and the establishment of import restrictions or import quotas which have the effect of sheltering a domestic industry or firm from unwarranted foreign competition. Government research and development programs often support the creation of a next generation of commercial products. Since the 1960s, MITI had supported very substantial funds for research into computers and semi-conductors. As this new technology reached the stage of transfer into industrial production, MITI used its administrative guidance to urge Japanese companies to get into the industry, and it fended off foreign involvement in the domestic market. Administrative guidance in this case also meant highly successful efforts to encourage the linking of computers and machine tools to produce robotized production capabilities, and to encourage the most advanced electronics in consumer products.

The national government has used its authority in the intergovernmental structure to establish industrial development programs for selected industries. Administrative guidance involves negotiating with local governments to set aside land for industrial development, and obtain commitments for the development of supporting infrastructure.

These examples of administrative guidance are largely drawn from MITI and economic development, but every ministry practices the art. It is how ministries function. Administrative guidance can be aggressive and dominating, or it can be timid and vacillating. It is not inherently good or evil, and may be wise or foolish according to circumstance and outcome. It is more a function of leadership and judgement about what is needed than it is the execution of some law or regulation. In economic matters, it seems clear that the Japanese are appalled by what they perceive to be the American pattern of confrontational government–private sector relationships, pursued through arm's-length adversarial regulation, or by high cost, high conflict enforcement and court-room litigation. To them, administrative guidance is preferable, and it works because there is a commonality of interest and intent. This is not seen as the corruption of government but as common sense — are not both working in the best interests of the country?

As Chalmers Johnson puts it:

> The power of administrative guidance greatly enhances the ability of Japanese economic officials to respond to new situations rapidly and with flexibility, and it gives them sufficient scope to take initiative. The Japanese have definitely profited from the elimination of legal middlemen and the avoidance of the adversarial relationship in public–private dealings.[3]

REGULATORY POWERS

The regulatory authorities of the government are so extensive and so complex that there is no simple comprehensive way to explain them. The following material is simply an attempt to list by ministry at least the major regulatory roles.

Summary of the Regulatory Roles of the Japanese National Government

Office of the Prime Minister

1. *The Fair Trade Commission*: (a) *The Trade Practices Department*: unfair trade practices; unjustifiable premiums; misleading advertising; prompt payments to contractors. (b) *The Economics Department*: review of mergers; international contracts and agree-

ments; matters relating to coordination of economic laws and orders.

2. *The Environmental Disputes Coordination Commission*: adjudication of environmental disputes; designation of areas where mining is prohibited.
3. *The Administration and Coordination Agency*: investigation of complaints against the performance of government agencies or corporations.
4. *The Science and Technology Agency*: *The Nuclear Safety Bureau*: the regulation of reactors, nuclear materials and radio-isotopes; prevention of other nuclear energy related hazards.
5. *The Environment Agency*: (a) *Nature Conservation Bureau*: enforcement of laws dealing with preservation of parks and other natural protected areas, wildlife protection, and hunting regulations. (b) *Air Quality Bureau*: environmental quality standards, enforcement of pollution laws, including noise, vibration, and offensive odors. (c) *Water Quality Bureau*: enforcement of water pollution standards, including ground subsidence, soil pollution, treatment of wastes from industrial, agricultural, and home sources.

Ministry of Justice

1. *Civil Affairs Bureau*: registration of property, registration of domestic and foreign corporations.
2. *Civil Liberties Bureau*: investigation and protection against violations of civil rights laws.
3. *Immigration Bureau*: regulation of the activities of alien visitors and residents.

Ministry of Finance

1. *Customs and Tariff Bureau*: assessment and collection of customs fees; control of export and import of goods; licensing of customhouse brokers.
2. *Securities Bureau*: regulation of securities registration and trading; licensing and supervision of securities exchanges and other securities investment institutions; standards for corporate accounting and auditing; registration of bonds.
3. *Banking Bureau*: supervision of the Bank of Japan; regulation of interest rates of financial institutions; supervision of the Deposit Insurance program; licensing of commercial banks, savings and loan companies, and credit associations; supervision of the

Export–Import Bank, the Japan Development Bank, and other government financial institutions; licensing of insurance businesses.

4. *International Finance Bureau*: control of foreign exchange transactions; authorization and inspection of foreign exchange banking.
5. *National Tax Administration Agency*: control of the production and sale of liquors; issuance of licenses to manufacturers or dealers of liquors.

Ministry of Education

1. *Elementary and Secondary Education Bureau*: review of the appointment of superintendents of boards of education of prefectures and major municipalities; authorization of textbooks.
2. *Higher Education Bureau*: approval of the establishment or discontinuance of universities and technical colleges; establishment of basic standards of higher education.
3. *Administration Bureau*: approval and authorization of school juridicial persons; establishment of basic standards for school facilities.

Ministry of Health and Welfare

1. *Medical Affairs Bureau*: enforcement of the Medical Service Law; regulatory guidance with respect to the professional qualifications and standards of performance for physicians, dentists, nurses, and others in medical care services; supervision of the operation of national hospitals and sanitoria.
2. *Pharmaceutical Affairs Bureau*: supervision of the pharmaceutical industry; supervision of the professional qualifications and standards of pharmacists; approval and registration of pharmaceutical preparations; control of narcotics, opium, marihuana, and poisonous and powerful drugs; approval and registration of biological and antibiotic products; control of inferior quality drugs; control of drug labeling.
3. *Health Insurance Bureau*: enforcement of the national health insurance program.
4. *Pension Bureau*: enforcement of the national pension program.

Ministry of Agriculture, Forestry, and Fisheries

1. *Livestock Industry Bureau*: quarantine of animals and animal products for import and export; guidance on livestock marketing.

2. *Food and Marketing Bureau*: consumer protection; labeling standards; standards for inspection of forestry, fishery, and vegetable products for export.
3. *The Food Agency*: inspection of agricultural products; granting of permits for the import or export of food products.
4. *The Forestry Agency*: inspection of forest products; inspection and protection of forests; inspection of forestry practices.
5. *The Fisheries Agency*: licensing of fishery operations in inland and coastal fisheries; regulation of fisheries operations by foreigners; regulation of fishing boat construction; registration of fishing boats.

Ministry of International Trade and Industry

1. *International Trade Administration Bureau*: control and inspection of exports; supervision of organizations related to foreign trade.
2. *Industrial Policy Bureau*: affairs concerning the protection of general consumer interests involving commodity exchanges, department stores, installment sales, control of prices, screening of foreign investors' acquisition of stocks.
3. *Industrial Location and Environmental Protection Bureau*: affairs concerning the prevention of pollution, treatment of industrial waste; control of explosives and high pressure gases; prevention of dangers in mines.
4. *Agency for Natural Resources and Energy*: licenses for the petroleum refining industry; investigation and compensation for damages from the coal mining industry; matters concerning the rates and supply of public utilities for gas and electricity.
5. *The Patent Office*: registration of industrial property rights, designs, trademarks, and the property rights of inventors.

Ministries of Transport

1. *Shipping Bureau*: licensing of passenger liner service; permits for coastal shipping; permits for lease or transfer of vessels; regulation of ocean-going vessel operation.
2. *Ship Bureau*: inspections of vessels, engines, and rigging.
3. *Seafarers Bureau*: certification of competency for mariners and the qualifications and manning concerning ship's officers.
4. *Ports and Harbors Bureau*: industrial standards for port facilities; approval of warehouse operations.

5. *Railway Supervision Bureau*: supervision of the production of railway equipment; permits for construction of new rail lines, or the transfer of lines; permits for the operations of railways or tram lines; fares and charges of railways and trolley buses; regulation of railway safety.
6. *Road Transport Bureau*: permits for motor transportation enterprises, motor roads, railway forwarding and clearing house enterprises; rates, fares, and charges for these businesses; registration and financing of motor vehicles; maintenance, inspection, and repair of motor vehicles; regulation of matters pertaining to vehicle insurance, operating practices, safety, and pollution.
7. *Civil Aviation Bureau*: licenses and permits pertaining to air transportation; fares and charges for air transportation; supervision and inspection of Japan Air Lines; inspection of air terminals; registration of aircraft; inspection of air navigational aids; airworthiness certification and inspection of aircraft; certification of pilots and other crew members and licensing of air traffic control facilities.
8. *Maritime Safety Agency*: enforcement of law and order at sea; control of rules of navigation and sailing; port regulations; marine pollution prevention.

Ministry of Posts and Telecommunications

1. *Telecommunications Policy Bureau*: regulation of the telecommunications industry; regulation and supervision of wire communications; regulation of computer communications.
2. *Radio Regulatory Bureau*: regulation of radio wavelengths and frequency allocation; permits for operation of radio stations; regulation of broadcast practices.

Ministry of Labor

1. *Labor Policy Bureau*: enforcement of trade union and labor protection laws, labor–management agreements, and operation of cooperatives and credit organizations.
2. *Labor Standards Bureau*: regulations concerning wages, hours, working conditions, workers' welfare, and safety of workplaces; workmen's compensation and insurance.
3. *Women's and Young Workers' Bureau*: enforcement of laws protecting these workers.
4. *Central Labor Relations Commission*: examination of cases of unfair labor practices; arbitration of labor disputes.

Ministry of Construction

1. *Planning Bureau*: environmental protection during construction; regulation of land use, land development, public use of land.
2. *River Bureau*: permits for water use; enforcement of measures for reclamation of public water areas.
3. *Road Bureau*: guidance with respect to construction and safety of roads and highways; supervision of tramway and motorway businesses.
4. *Housing Bureau*: supervision of public use housing; control of land rents and house rents; licensing of architects; regulation of slum clearance projects.

Ministry of Home Affairs

1. *Local Administration Bureau*: oversight over the establishment and management of local governments; standards for local administration and personnel management; review and approval of local government plans, budgets; supervision of election management; permission for local bond issues.

In many instances, these regulatory powers are shared with local governments, in an interlocking network of regulatory authority. The usual pattern is for the national government to issue a basic law which establishes general regulatory authority. This is supplemented by second-level laws which detail specific cases such as air quality protection, selection of school textbooks, standards for child labor protection, or licensing of banks. Responsibility for each regulation is assigned to one of the national ministries which further elaborates it, either through more detailed regulations, or through administrative guidance. Prefectures and municipalities are almost always granted by statute the right to participate in the formulation of a regulatory policy, or of a course of implementing action stemming from that authority. The operational implementation of a regulation may be delegated to a prefecture, and it may then exercise an additional degree of latitude or administrative guidance of its own.

Prefectures also have a level of regulatory authority of their own directly given them by the Local Autonomy Law, and their regulatory role is often a combination of both direct and delegated responsibility. For example, in matters of environmental protection, prefectures are participants and commentors in the development of national guidelines for pollution prevention plans and in the Cabinet-level determination of which areas will be designated as high concentration pollution areas needing special anti-pollution control measures. Prefectures may then be delegated responsibilities such as the processing and payment of claims for environmental damage, or the licensing of companies in every aspect of environmental hygiene, or waste disposal.

Under their direct authority, prefectures can pass by-laws which set local standards for the use and shipment of harmful substances, or which deal with drainage systems, or which determine local water quality standards and protections. They may also grant licenses for the operation of waste disposal facilities and set regulatory standards to control the disposal. As part of its responsibilities for the supervision of a national industrial development project, a prefecture may exercise substantial regulatory control over industrial companies in meeting the requirements of the development project, or in compliance with national or local regulations of all kinds.

Prefectures play a key role in the regulatory aspects of land use policy. They are participants in all national government plans or programs for land improvement, soil conservation, coastal zone protection, pollution protection, or land subsidence prevention. They may directly regulate the use of lands for certain kinds of agriculture, or for urban infrastructure purposes, such as road access, zoning, or preemption for public facilities.

Both prefectures and municipalities are the source of many forms of licenses and permits to operate, such as for pipelines or refineries, local TV or radio broadcasting, housing construction, and most commercial businesses.

Both levels of local government are also authorized to license and inspect many professional and technical people, including doctors, dentists, medical and dental technicians and hygienists, pharmacists, food service personnel, barbers, electricians, and many others.

FUTURE DIRECTIONS

Strangely, the Japanese seem to prefer the vagaries of administrative guidance to the precision of regulation. The Provisional Commission on Administrative Reform recommends that the trend for the future of regulation should be two-fold: first, there should be a drawing back and reduction of those regulations which are unnecessarily constraining on the freedom of the private sector, and this ought, in its judgement, to include the elimination of licenses by government which are bureaucratic permission to exist. The Commission has attempted to present the philosophy that governments should become involved in private sector affairs not routinely, but on an exception basis when it can be established that some impairment of the general public good is occurring, and this view is likely to achieve wider recognition.

Second, the Commission believes that independence is good between governments as well, and came out as a strong advocate of the elimination of a large proportion of the enormously detailed administrative apparatus which the national government imposes through its very detailed laws, and its administrative controls. The local autonomy movement strongly favors this concept, and hopes that the views of the Commission will start to break the inertia which exists in the central ministries.

Notes

1.   "Japan: Environmentalism with Growth", *Wall Street Journal*, September 5, 1980.
2.   Johnson (1982: 273).
3.   Johnson (1982: 273).

9 The Intertwining of Government and Industry: the Case of the Transportation System

Japan is a country in which it is literally impossible to tell for certain where its government leaves off and its private sector begins. This chapter will attempt briefly to describe this interrelationship primarily from the perspective of the deployment of government power and how that power creates conditions in which government and private companies are parts of a complex matrix in which almost no decision can be said to be made solely by one or the other. Even a superficial examination of the role of the government shows a power so great that one becomes aware that it could be dictatorial and corrosive if improperly exercised. This creates the need to understand if possible why it is not, and how the interplay of forces has taken place to produce results which must be considered both effective and reasonably democratic.

Understanding the respective roles of government and industry in the transportation sector requires a brief digression back into Japanese economic history. Earlier in this book, the dominance of the national government was emphasized, partly in terms of the central strategy of rapid heavy industrialization. During the 1930s control of the government began to slip into the hands of a coalition of the military and a cadre of "new bureaucrats" who believed that Japan could not survive and succeed in becoming a first-rate world power unless it was prepared to develop the force to dominate its sources of raw materials and, in the last analysis, take what it needed by force if necessary. As this group moved into power it increasingly used the authorities of the central government to set national priorities aimed at building a strong military establishment. Top priority was given to oil, coal, electric power, steel, munitions, and ocean shipping. Governmental techniques were devised which cultivated the ability to create national strategic economic plans, subsidizing selected key industries, and forcing the creation of the public infrastructure and the relocation of people to become the new urban industrial workforce.

The occupation of Manchuria trained a cadre of military officers and key bureaucrats in the skills of economic development for a whole country, and many of the same people and the same techniques began to move into similar roles in the homeland itself.[1] The protracted and inconclusive war with China had the effect of extending and solidifying the role of the military in the central government, and in forcing private companies to move in the direction of a militarized economy. This in turn was only possible through very extensive neglect of the needs of the civilian population.

These trends, however disastrous in their immediate consequences, nevertheless created a mentality for pervasive economic planning which carried over into the post-war era and became vital then as well. Japan was compelled by its defeat, by war-time destruction, and by the repeated near-collapse of its economy to adapt these centralist economic planning and management skills to revitalize its economic apparatus.

This in turn has created a national government in which the roles are almost always more comprehensive and more penetrating than those of its US counterpart. This can be well understood by a panoramic look at the major elements of the national transportation system.

BROAD ECONOMIC PLANNING

Transportation is an important part of the total industrial/commercial base of the country, and the key element in the formulation of overall industrial strategy has been in the hands of the Ministry of International Trade and Industry (MITI) since its creation in 1949 as the successor of the Ministry of Commerce and Industry. Chalmers Johnson describes in fascinating detail the enormous influence of MITI policies on the economy, and the extraordinary pace with which it rose from the ashes of defeat and became the "miracle" economy of the world. To quote from Johnson[2] the Japanese "model" for economic achievement has four principal elements:

1. "... a small, inexpensive, but elite bureaucracy, staffed by the best *managerial* talent in the system.
2. ... a political system in which the bureaucracy is given sufficient scope to take the initiative and operate effectively.
3. ... State intervention in the economy.
4. ... a pilot organization like MITI."

As Johnson sees the Japanese experience, the private sector and the government were fully convinced that each needed the other, and that a sufficient degree of trust could be sustained to permit effective cooperation. This did not mean that conflict would not occur, but rather that if both adhered to a general commitment to pursue market-conforming policies, conflict would become negotiation and compromise out of which a substantial agreement on an agenda of action would emerge.

This combination of forces in the private sector and the government establishment assured the general cooperation of the LDP and the Diet which provided the political environment for conceding great scope and authority to MITI. In addition, one of the principal functions of this political backing has been to fend off or modulate pressures from other elements of Japanese society where it was felt that these might deter or impair the critical elements of the economic development agenda.

Under this political umbrella, it has been the duty of the MITI bureaucracy, as Johnson put it,[3] "first, to identify and choose the industries to be developed; second, to identify and choose the best means of rapidly developing the chosen industries; and third, to supervise the competition in the designated strategic sectors in order to guarantee their economic health and effectiveness."

MITI thus emerged as an institution of special characteristics and strengths in the Japanese development state. It has played the lead role in the development of priority elements of the transportation system such as shipbuilding prior to and after the war, and the emergence of the automobile manufacturing industry. Government economic policies in the mid-1960s sought to enlarge Japanese corporate entities so that they could be more competitive with foreign companies (which seems almost laughable after the fact), and to prevent takeover or majority investment by foreigners. The steel industry was actually consolidated under a plan of this kind, and there was a MITI plan which would have consolidated nine auto firms

(Daihatsu, Fuji, Honda, Hino, Isuzu, Mitsubishi, Nissan, Suzuki, Toyo Kogyo, and Toyota) down to just Nissan and Toyota. There was a fierce struggle within the bureaucracy, with the Economic Development Agency supporting MITI, but serious opposition from the Fair Trade Commission, which is the defender of Japan's weak anti-trust laws. The Fair Trade Commission was fighting out of its class, and it is generally believed that this merger would have been ordered, but in a relatively rare instance of a corporation defying MITI's "administrative guidance", the huge Mitsubishi Corporation struck a deal in 1969 with Chrysler Corporation to manufacture Dodge Colts and Plymouth Champs for the American market. Mitsubishi was backed by most of the other auto companies which had deals of their own in mind, and their combined strength and political influence overwhelmed MITI in what was perhaps its worst policy defeat. The Japanese government equivocated until 1971, but the deal went through, and MITI was never quite the same.

MITI continues to be the ministry which shapes and directs the general pattern of economic development, and this has meant that it has laid down the groundrules for the development of highway networks, airport locations, harbor and port development and other transportation infrastructure. It even contributes government capital financing to the Nihon Airplane Manufacturing Company Limited, so that Japan has at least one domestic manufacturer of aircraft for the military and for small commercial and private planes, although Mitsubishi also produces such aircraft.

But the bulk of the relationships with the transportation sector are pursued through the Ministry of Transport (MOT). As with most national ministries, MOT sees itself as "in charge" of its industry, and its roles include industry development and support, much research and education, and industry regulation. The Japanese reject the need for separation of development and regulation, and think that the American propensity for independent regulatory agencies is both unwarranted and dangerous.

MARITIME AFFAIRS

As befits Japan's role as an island nation and one of the major seafaring countries in the world, the government, for a hundred years, has maintained a compelling presence in maritime affairs, and MOT is heavily weighted in this area.

Shipping and Ship Construction

The ministry's role is both developmental and regulatory. The Shipping Bureau is responsible for the development of the shipbuilding industry and it can make loans for construction of ocean-going vessels or pay the interest on private loans as a form of construction subsidy. MOT approves the private construction of vessels, and their lease, transfer, or overseas sale. It regulates the operation of vessels in international trade, and of coastal shipping and the operation of passenger carrying vessels. It further issues regulations which control the safety elements of ship design and operation and it inspects both ships and equipment to make sure they are operating safely. The Japan Shipbuilding Industry Foundation is a government corporation created to promote the advancement of the industry, and there is a "Council for the Rationalization of Shipping and Shipbuilding Industries" which allows private firms to coordinate their intentions without violation of anti-trust laws. The ministry also partly supervises another government corporation, the Japan Nuclear Research and Development Agency, which has designed and constructed vessels with nuclear reactor power systems.

During the 1950s and '60s, Japan was the premier shipbuilding country in the world, but cheaper labor forces in South Korea, Taiwan, and elsewhere successfully captured much of the new ship construction. In addition, there was and is a glut of vessels in international trade, and this element of Japanese economic development was deliberately allowed to decline. Unlike the Americans, the Japanese have very modest national security requirements for ships, and thus they have no need to subsidize domestic ship construction if it is not competitive.

The ministry is also the home for seamen's affairs. It is in charge of maritime labor relations, and it sets forth national regulations which protect seamen's working conditions, and pays compensation for accidents and injuries. It sets standards for programs of worker compensation including employee benefits. Finally, it issues certificates of competence for seamen and vessel officers, sets manning levels for ship operation, and provides education and training programs of all kinds. It directly operates an Institute for Sea Training, seamen's training schools, and a safety academy.

Ports and Harbors

Even in an era of bullet trains and super highways, Japan has a remarkably active and important coastal shipping network which is cheap and carries a high proportion of freight for many industries. MOT has authority to construct and operate port and harbor facilities where they are public works of national priority, and it can aid local communities in port development and operation. This may include the development of shore-side facilities such as docks, warehouses, loading and unloading equipment, and the dredging of harbor channels. This phases into other responsibilities for the reclamation of land and the development of drainage projects, and the issuance of regulations and policies which define the general use of public waters. And, of course, MOT regulates all of these activities.

Maritime Safety

The Japanese equivalent of the US Coast Guard is called the Maritime Safety Agency. It provides emergency search and rescue services and maintains navigational aids in coastal and inland waters. In addition, it develops navigational aids, hydrographic research and ship technology development, and operates the Maritime Safety Academy.

There is also an independent Marine Accident Inquiry Agency which does accident investigation on both the high seas and in coastal waters.

The Meteorological Agency provides maritime weather service, but it is also a broadly based research organization in meteorology, aerology, seismology, and marine ecology.

RAILWAYS

Japan's private railways slug it out with the trucking industry and cheap coastal shipping in order to survive in the freight movement business, and practically nobody cares. The unchallenged bright star of Japanese railroading for decades has been the Japanese National Railways (JNR) and its "Shinkansen" bullet trains, propelling its passengers in comfort at speeds up to 120 miles per hour, arriving at each station dead on time, and stopping so that each door opens at precisely marked positions on the platform. The bullet trains are a marvel of modern railroading and the standard of the world.

But the JNR is also a government corporation and it comes under the jurisdiction of the MOT. The ministry has both development and regulatory responsibilities for railways similar to those it has in maritime affairs. It encourages and sometimes assists in the development and manufacture of railroad rolling stock and buses; and it sets safety and operating regulations for freight and passenger services, subways, transit but services, and even tramways. It also regulates bus and rail operation and equipment maintenance.

Through grants and subsidies, MOT can support the development of additional rail and bus services and mass transit as part of urban or regional development plans. At the same time, the ministry is an economic regulator, since it sets rates and charges for various elements of the industry.

Railroads were introduced in Japan in the 1870s, and early lines were initially developed by the government, often over the stubborn resistance of many elements in society. Private railroads began to develop soon after, but the government has always been ambivalent about the feasibility and adequacy of private rail service. Many railroads were nationlized as early as 1907, and from that time until the present there has always been one or more state-owned railroads, culminating in the current JNR, operating as a government corporation.

The JNR is an excellent lesson in the political and financial problems which confront a minister of state. JNR has been such an important and impressive public service that it has become a political "sacred cow", almost impervious to ministerial "guidance". But beginning about 1965, JNR has been operating at a big deficit, now running in excess of a trillion yen per year; and this deficit must be explained and defended by the minister in successive budgets which, since 1975, have also been heavily in deficit. Every Minister of Transport for the last 20 years has been charged with attempting to constrain JNR's ambitious plans for expansion of service and ever more bullet trains.

What is little realized, however, is that the role of the MOT includes the development and well-being of private railroads as well, and grants and subsidies have helped them to prosper. Japan has been both wise and fortunate in the development of its rail passenger system. The population density is great, and is concentrated in dense corridors of urban areas on the coastal plains, and there is a high level of inter-city travel. The MOT and other elements of the government wisely committed to development of rail travel and the rail system was well embedded in society before the impact of the auto/highway combination which ruined inter-city rail travel and urban mass transit in the United States.

During the last few years, the success of private rail carriers has increasingly given the government the potential for an alternative to the JNR. The recommendations of the Nakasone Provisional Commission on Administrative Reform have provided the political leverage for a change of policy under which the MOT will now supervise the breaking up of JNR into a number of regional systems. For the first time in history Japan may be on the verge of a rail passenger network which is entirely private.

There is a further lesson in public administration in the JNR story. It illustrates the fact that the MOT sees itself as responsible for the whole rail industry, and did not feel that it was forced to defend the JNR as a government corporation against its private competitors. As it became clear that private railroads could out-compete JNR, ministerial strategic planning was perfectly capable of moving toward privatization, even of its star performer.

CIVIL AVIATION

In part because of the greater geographical concentration of its urban areas and in part because of the superior rail system, Japan has never developed the same level of civil aviation usage as in the US. It has only two private domestic air carriers certified for operation by the MOT — All Nippon Airways and Toa Domestic Airlines — which monopolize domestic air travel. It has had just one international air carrier, Japan Air Lines, which also operates as a private corporation, but has government capital funding in it.[4] Like its US counterpart, the Federal Aviation Administration (FAA), the Civil Aviation Bureau regulates the industry by setting safety standards and inspecting airline operations and maintenance. It issues airworthiness certificates for aircraft and certifies pilots and crews. It also acts as an economic regulator because it sets fares and charges. In its development role it is a principal source of public funds for airport construction, improvement, and operations. Also like FAA, it operates the air traffic control system. Many airports are operated by local airport authorities.

MOT negotiates international aviation agreements and bilateral agreements with other countries for the establishment of international air routes, landing rights, and fare structures. The Civil Aviation Bureau runs the New Tokyo International Airport at Norita, which serves the Tokyo metropolitan area. The airport is actually run by another government corporation, with partial funding from local governments. (Recently the US Congress legislated the creation of a corporation to run Dulles and Washington National airports, administered by the state of Virginia and the District of Columbia.)

HIGHWAYS AND ROAD TRANSPORT

The one important exception to the authority of the MOT in the transportation sector is the construction and maintenance of the national highway and road system. This authority has long been in the Ministry of Construction (MOC) because it is the policy to place all kinds of major construction into a single technical ministry, and also because MOC is generally responsible for the infrastructure elements of urban and regional planning, of which the transportation network is a key part.

MOC also functions through a series of government corporations which have the latitude to operate like private businesses. The Japan Highway Corporation plans and constructs the major national highway network, and a special Metropolitan Expressway Corporation does the same thing for expressway systems in and around large urban complexes. On very large, complex, long-term projects, such as the network in the Tokyo region, special single-purpose corporations have been created. The ministry also constructs and operates toll roads and major bridges such as the Honshu-Shikoku Bridge Authority which operates a network of bridges which connect the two islands.

There is a secondary and local road network which is the responsibility of the prefectures, and for which financing is shared. Here again, government corporations have been created to do the actual construction and maintenance, and they are supervised by the governor of each prefecture who has the authority to approve their plans and budgets. The whole system is planned and largely financed by the national ministry, but both governors and city mayors are given the right to participate in, and sometimes approve, the selection of road routes, design, construction of toll roads and bridges, and standards for safety and maintenance.

The principal role of the Ministry of Transport with respect to highway transportation is as a regulator of highway use. The ministry grants permits and franchises to operate to trucking companies, passenger bus services, freight forwarders, and freight terminals. It is also the economic regulator of these industries through the setting of rates and fees for freight carriage. It has authority to set safety standards for the operation of all of these facilities and to inspect them and order improvements. It delegates to prefectures, which may in turn delegate to municipalities, the authority to register motor vehicles and to register auto mortgages. There is also an inspection of cars and trucks to make sure that they are properly maintained and that they meet strict emission control standards, and carry adequate insurance.

TRANSPORTATION TAXES

The transportation system relies heavily on special "user charge" taxes to finance its own development. As in the US, there is a gasoline tax and other special taxes on aviation fuel, local road use, and a tonnage tax on ports, and these are all transferred to local governments for their use. The entire local road tax is transferred, with two-thirds to prefectures, and one-third to municipalities. There is also a motor vehicle tonnage tax, 25% of which goes to cities.

About 15% of the aviation fuel tax goes to cover the costs of certain designated airports, and cities get about 80% of this money. Finally, the port tonnage tax goes entirely to those cities which have designated ports, and is not earmarked but may be used for any kind of port or harbor development or operation expense. In addition to these national taxes, prefectures levy a motor vehicle and an auto purchase tax, and cities also tax auto registration and can apply a local gas tax as well.

In summary, all elements of the transportation system are, with minor exceptions, part of national responsibilities because they are seen as crucial elements in top-down national strategies for industrial development and urbanization. The national government has been willing to consult with local governments, and may make concessions to local interests, but would not tolerate the degree of local option which is a normal right for local governments in the United States.

Nor will the government tolerate much unconstrained and undirected private sector initiative either, and it has frequently acted through its regulatory powers to determine the size, composition, and policy of private companies. The price for this centralist control has come in the form of substantial national budgets for transportation capability and often, as in the case of the JNR, at a high level of subsidy cost to sustain the public will. The Ministries of Transport and Construction are both among the most significant users of the government corporations as a means to carry out construction and other "businesslike" operations, and as a result they will be particularly hard hit in the new wave of "privatization" precipitated by Prime Minister Nakasone.

Notes

1. Most of this discussion is based on Johnson's marvellous book *MITI and the Japanese Miracle: The Growth of Industrial Policy, 1925–1975* (1982).
2. Johnson (1982) pp. 315–319.
3. Johnson (1982) p. 315.
4. In 1986, All Nippon Airlines was licensed for limited international carriage.

10 Central Guidance of a Decentralized Public Service: the Case of the Education System

There is nothing in their whole society that gives such clear insights into the Japanese character as their education system. When the Japanese finally decided to educate their whole population, they did so with a drive and zeal and degree of commitment which was awesome. The corporate world has not been the sole creators of a race of over-achievers. It has really been one of the grateful beneficiaries of a school system which is one of the most structured and demanding in the world. But that system is also one in which stress is deliberately applied to five-year-olds, and 15-year-olds are confronted with "make or break" decisions that can affect their entire lives.

Why do the Japanese put such pressure on their children? It's hard to understand from the outside of the society, and apparently not that much easier from the inside. Japan has had a strong tradition of respect for learning, derived from Chinese influences, but this doesn't explain much. The government has made education a national priority for more than 100 years but, unlike the transportation system discussed in the last chapter, governments are not the compelling force which drives the education system. The investment of public funds for education is sufficient, but not exceptional by world standards. Teachers seem to be competent and respected, but instruction centers around uniform packages of standard educational material and not individual exceptional teaching.

What really appears to be the driving force in education is that still largely unexplained zealousness in Japanese society which drives them to achieve and to excel at whatever they do. Japanese education is neither a philosophical contemplation of knowledge nor a fuzzy exercise to cultivate individual creativity. At levels up to college, it is a **production system** — a hard, unremitting production process, with very high outputs and quality control standards, aimed at producing a large population of highly "fact literate" young adults who will take their place in a society which is also hard driving and pointed toward a Japanese role and presence in the world which is not clear, but must be superior.

As with so many other elements of society, World War II and the post-war Constitution are clear watersheds in the evolution of the education system. The difference between pre-war and post-war conceptions is like looking at two different nations with two different and diametrically opposed views on the value and purpose of education.

Despite the real tradition for learning, education before the war was seen as the privilege and the tool of the elite. For example, a survey of 1905 showed that there was a reasonable 1% of the population which held university degrees, but this was at a time when only 4.3% of the population had even completed secondary education! Education was for an elitist bureaucracy, for industrialists and necessary cadres of technical experts, and for a portion of the aristocracy which, like the British, were being prepared for what they regarded as their natural right to lead the country. Even as late as the 1930s, secondary school completion had advanced only to about 32% and university degrees to 3%. These numbers are not out of line with the experience of other advanced countries, but they did reflect the inertia of an elitist view which frustrated a broader public yearning for education.

During the post-war period, the growth in these numbers was absolutely explosive, particularly at the elementary and secondary level. By 1970 87% of the population were completing secondary education and 19% were obtaining university degrees. By 1985 these numbers were 97% and 33% respectively. It has been estimated that, for Japanese people over 55 years of age, only 8% have had higher education, but that number is 40% for the 25–35-year-old bracket. The trigger for this educational explosion was clearly the Constitution which mandated free, compulsory education (for girls too) through six years of elementary instruction and three years of "lower secondary" education, and began a public commitment of investment in teachers and educational facilities which has lasted for 20 years, and which, in modified form, is still going on.

THE STRUCTURE OF ELEMENTARY AND SECONDARY EDUCATION

Like almost every other public program, the educational system looks like it had been designed by an engineer rather than an artist, a politician, or even an educator. Only this time, the structure and service delivery responsibilities are highly delegated into the local government structure, and the national government does not exercise the same degree of "clout" that it does in other programs. The public school system is run by municipalities, as shown in Table 10.1.

Table 10.1:   Provision of Schools

Type	National	Local	Private
Kindergarten	48	6,197	8,907
Elementary	73	24,802	168
Lower secondary	77	10,252	550
Upper secondary	17	3,954	1,242
Technical college	54	4	4
Junior college	36	51	439
University	95	34	326
Special training	189	159	2,456
Miscellaneous	9	141	4,717

Public schools are municipally run, except for kindergartens, which are optional in the system and are in fact privately operated. Many parents pay extra to send their children to kindergarten to give them a little edge in the long competition which follows. The system follows the 6–3–3–4 structure adapted from the United States; that is, there is a six-year elementary level and a three-year lower secondary level which constitute the required free basic education mandated by the Constitution, plus three more years of upper secondary instruction and four years of university.

All children must take the initial nine years of education. It is single track, with few options, and it consists of a standard "package" of instruction defined by the national Ministry of Education, Science, and Culture (MESC), after extensive consultation and advice from all elements of the professional education community.

The standard package includes Japanese language, social studies, arithmetic, science, music, arts, handicrafts, home-making, and physical education. There is a standard "Course of Study" which spells out a second and third level of specifics for each of these subjects by semester, as well as very carefully defined sets of objectives for each.

No significant digression is permitted from the Course of Study. The whole education community from the Ministry on down is committed to the view that this package of instruction is as complete and useful as their professional judgement can make it, and that it constitutes what each student must learn in order to master the subject. Class hours are long; they run five-and-a-half days a week, and there is only a brief vacation of a little over a month in summer, and short breaks at New Year and before the beginning of the new school year in April. Instruction is intense and fact-laden; and every boy and a girl is expected to complete the work. Discipline is strict, but morale is kept high. If some students are less able to absorb the instruction, teachers take pride in working with them and giving them special help, and in fact, there are few failures.

The first major crisis point in the system comes at the completion of the mandatory nine years of instruction. In theory, all students are eligible for progression into the upper elementary grades which are the equivalent of the upper three years of high school in the United States. But entrance into these grades is by competitive examination, and flexibility is available for students to seek out and apply to the best schools. This step, therefore, has become a highly competitive process, and the results of the competition can make or blight a child's whole future.

There is a sort of "self-fulfilling prophecy" at work in this process, because "better" schools tend to be those whose graduates compete for and win places in the "better" universities. But once a high school becomes known as a better school, it tends to draw the best and brightest students who write better exams, which, in turn, is the real basis for selection by the top universities.

Progress beyond lower secondary education into high school and in turn into either a public or private university is strictly by competitive examination, and this flow is the mainstream of Japanese education. Thus, obtaining high scores on entrance exams has become the compelling preoccupation for the majority of students. Much of their future rides on the results because that's the way society wants it. Both industry and government hire from high schools and universities by examination, and the best paid and most promising and prestigious jobs go to the best students from the best schools. For example, the best students entering the national government are from the University of Tokyo or one or two other top-level universities, and they tend to enter the Ministry of Finance or MITI. Graduates of provincial universities who want to go into government will probably have to wait to hear from the Ministry of Posts and Telecommunications or even the Ministry of Education, Science, and Culture.

This mainstream system appears from the outside to be confining and somehow old fashioned, and yet it is very rich in knowledge and it does develop in young people powerful learning capabilities and a discipline of study and mastery of knowledge which is of extraordinary value in future life. And this is not just "business education". The curriculum through twelve grades includes work in science, art, literature, and music. While it is hard to make comparative judgements, Japanese students probably rank first in the world in mathematics attainment, and are in the upper reaches of such diverse fields as science and music. It is usual for most Japanese students to learn to play and enjoy one of more musical instruments and the general national level of musical literacy is perhaps the highest in the world.

But what happens to the student who is not able to follow this mainstream? To their credit, the Japanese are reluctant to give up further education for those who are not headed for the top. The philosophy of national education policy is a commitment to lifetime learning, and the role of the national government is actually more direct in some of the alternative streams of education and training than it is in the mainstream described above.

GOVERNMENT STRUCTURE FOR EDUCATION

As with other government programs, the basis of the educational system was defined in national laws which mandate the roles of prefectures and municipalities. The basic statute is the Fundamental Law of Education (1947) which lays down general aims for creating a "culture of mutual esteem and cooperation"[1] that respects academic freedom and requires the State and local public bodies to establish and maintain schools and "give them every financial assistance."[2] Teachers, like all public employees are "servants of the whole community"[3] and education must be equally available to all "according to ability, without regard to race, creed, sex, social status, economic position, or family origin". For many years, the Ministry of Education included an Agency for Cultural Affairs, and in fact, in

1983, the name of the Ministry was changed to Education, Science, and Culture.

The Japanese quite attractively seek to link education and culture together. They believe strongly in the preservation of their own cultural heritage and see education of the young as the best strategy to perpetuate and encourage that heritage. This ministry promotes the diffusion of the arts, architecture, national monuments and shrines, and religious and cultural sites and knowledge. It also may make grants for these purposes, and administers historical and cultural properties, and collections of works of art.

Table 10.2 which shows the distribution of education funds reveals a number of important facts about the system. It shows that, while most elementary and secondary schools are run by the municipalities, funding is shared between the three levels of government. The heavy funding from prefectures is largely explained by the fact that they essentially control and direct school systems, under the technical guidance of prefectural education commissions, and have accepted responsibility for paying almost all of the salaries and benefits of teachers.

The national government share of finance for the compulsory nine grades is essentially a subsidy, and the ministry does not attempt to dictate the actions of schools as other national ministries do in so many other programs. Funds from the national government and receipts from various forms of tuition are paid to the prefectures which control them.

Taking another look at Table 10.1, it is clear that the national government takes a special interest in certain institutions which tend to handle those students who do not flow through the mainstream of general high school to four-year universities.

At the high school level there is in fact a second stream. Forty-eight percent of these schools offer only the general curriculum, but about 23% offer both that and a vocational education program, and the remaining 23% are "vocational education only" institutions. Vocational education has a long and honorable history, growing out of older, simpler times when there was less expectation that such a large number of students would go on to a university. The vocational education schools offer a number of special programs including industrial skills, commerce, agriculture, fisheries, home economics, health care, and the merchant marine. In addition, beginning at this level in both the general and vocational education programs, there are either special schools or special programs for the blind, deaf, or

Table 10.2: Educational Funds by Source

Source	Total	Compulsory	Special	Upper	Univs.	Other
National government	26	33	29	2	2	–
Prefectures	42	31	64	80	65	17
Municipalities	24	29	3	6	3	83
Tuitions	2	–	–	9	56	17
Other	6	7	4	3	–	–

Note: Tuition payments offset government expenditure.

those with other handicaps, and the national government runs such programs directly, or makes special grants and subsidies to assure their adequacy at the local government level.

There is also a layer of junior colleges which again tend to receive students who are unable to pursue the mainstream. These junior colleges are a logical extension of the vocational education high schools. Of these 83% are private, their student body can be as high as 90% female, and they tend to be heavily involved in "gender" education and training. The national government finances almost 36% of these programs.

Finally, there are special technical colleges which have been established to expand training in civil, mechanical, and electrical engineering, electronics, industrial chemistry, and other technical areas mainly of interest to industry. Here again this is a national government program with 54 out of 62 colleges directly operated by the national government which provides 87% of the funding. The national government also provides student loans. While this program has real values of its own, it is at least partially another option for students who are not able to follow the mainstream course of education.

UNIVERSITIES

The universities are entirely different in their style of operation than the hard-driving packaged education of the elementary and secondary schools. They are very much more in the tradition of their European and American counterparts, with independent faculties loosely organized into departments and schools; there is a minimum of direction in the shape of the curriculum, with each professor free to offer his or her own view of what students should receive, and there is very little direction or administrative control of departments by university administration. However, entrance is by competitive examination and this perpetuates the very pronounced and rigid "pecking order" ranking of institutions, which is strictly adhered to and creates intense competition for acceptance by the "better" universities.

There are now 455 universities, 255 of which offer graduate degrees. As shown in Table 10.1, 95 of these are national universities, and 34 are maintained by prefectures, but most are private institutions. The reputation of these institutions is very curious. As summarized by former Ambassador Reischauer:[4]

> The pecking order of universities remains essentially what it was before the war. Tokyo University still ranks far at the top and after it, the other former Imperial Universities (the term "Imperial" was dropped after the war), and a few specialized pre-war national universities such as Hitotsubashi for economics. Next comes the two most prestigious private universities, Keio and Waseda, and the national universities that were founded in each prefecture after the war by combining former high schools and higher technical schools and upgrading them. Next comes the great mass of private schools, divided into several prestige levels, and at the bottom are the junior colleges. The strict correlation between university affiliation and jobs in later life is gradually breaking down, but even today the great bulk of the higher bureaucracy comes from the most prestigious national universities, particularly Tokyo, while Keio is noted as a source of business executives, Waseda as a producer of politicians and journalists, and the less distinguished private universities pour out the masses of also-rans, who become the lesser businessmen and white collar workers.

The national universities thus attract many of the best students, who pay very reasonable tuitions. But the private universities are in a much weaker position. Education is expensive and, since public financial support is minimal, relatively high fees must be charged. This means that the best rated schools tend also to be the least expensive. There is a national policy for subsidization of private universities which provides help both for the purchase of facilities and equipment and for current operating expenses. While the policy proposes a 50% level of assistance for operating costs, the realities of deficit budgeting has kept this figure to around 20%.

On the whole, Japanese universities do not enjoy the same exceptional reputation for excellence as the elementary and secondary schools. But the pattern seems not unlike the US in that there are a relatively small number of universities which are of outstanding capability in one or two fields and generally excellent overall, but a very large number of institutions which are generally mediocre, and weak in many faculties, so that the education of even their brightest graduates is questionable.

Commenters with better insights about the university system see universities as almost a period of "coasting" between the intense elementary/secondary program and the selection of one's ultimate career. The entrance exams channel energy and intellectual attention into a species of cramming on nitty gritty. Faculties are seen as far less interested in actual teaching, and do not often take the same kind of personal interest in students and their problems as their secondary school associates. Government expenditures are generally low and tight-fisted. The national government spends less on its universities (2%) than it does on its technical colleges (3%). While professors are generally accorded much prestige and status in society, their pay is low and many become preoccupied with other income-generating activities, such as consulting and book publication.

There is a relatively low level of advanced academic research, partly because sources of funds are limited, and partly because graduate schools see themselves primarily as preparing candidates for academic careers and not for sophisticated research. It is also true and probably significant that a large proportion of private corporations and even government agencies have fairly sophisticated programs of further education for their promising employees, which often involve special higher education in highly regarded universities in other countries of the kind which will advance their knowledge of the world beyond the capacities of Japanese universities.

The MESC is fully aware of these problems, but is not really in a position to do much about them. The tradition of academic independence obviously precludes any massive government intervention into educational policy or substance, and there is little likelihood of any significant increase in the level of government funding, even if policy would permit it. In fact, its major policy objectives for the next ten years deal with these problems, but in indirect ways. The policy position is to oppose any expansion in the numbers of universities, including private ones, so that available aid can be concentrated on quality improvements rather than institution-building. Along with this is a policy to concentrate less on institutions in the large cities and attempt to build up and improve the quality of prefectural universities and schools in smaller communities. There are also plans for greater support for experiments in educational approaches, including greater latitude for students to take courses in universities other than their own, and the assisted introduction of new priority fields of study such as certain areas of scientific research and computer mathematics.

Perhaps the most attractive form of government involvement is the program of student scholarships. Such government programs are administered at the national level by the Japan Scholarship Foundation, but there are other programs offered by prefectures, municipalities, and some non-government sources.

The Japan Scholarship Foundation program is based on a concept of economic equality. That is, it provides loan scholarships mainly for high ranking students who are financially unable to continue their own education. The Foundation has two different programs: ordinary loans to any student who can demonstrate financial need; and a special program in which higher value loans are made to students of exceptional ability.

In the 40 years in which this scholarship aid has been available, almost 4.5 million students have benefited in amounts varying from 7,000 to 70,000 yen per month for doctoral candidates (at 160 yen per dollar, this would be from $44 to $438/month).

THE PUBLIC ADMINISTRATION OF EDUCATION

The legal basis for the public school system is set forth in a pattern which must be very apparent to anybody who has made it this far into this book: a broad enabling statute — the Fundamental Law of Education — enacted in 1947, which sets forth the concepts of free public education for nine grades, the principles of academic freedom, and of equal opportunity for all. A national Ministry of Education, Science, and Culture supervises the system and defines its further laws and regulations. A more detailed School Education Law is the basic definitional statute which sets forth the various levels of schools and the other elements of the structure of the system. There are special statutes which define and control in further detail standards for such things as class size, a table of organization for both teachers and administrative staff, and the provision of textbooks and other instructional material. There is another law which defines a whole special personnel program for teachers which includes standards for qualification, selection, certification, retention and promotion, salaries, and the kind and level of benefits, which are paid through a state supported and controlled teachers' mutual aid association.

But beyond this usual base of enabling statute, the MESC takes a more modest role in the stewardship of the system than is usual for national ministries. While the MESC does oversee the system and has very strong latent administrative powers, in fact, the center of gravity through the upper secondary level is with the prefectures. The MESC confines itself mainly to the establishment of uniform administrative groundrules for the operation of schools, curricula, preparation of educational materials, and some educational research. It provides review, advice, and modest "administrative guidance" to prefectures and in turn may require a range of plans, reports, data, and budget estimates.

The prefectures exercise the real control over the system. They establish school districts, approve budgets subject to final MESC concurrence, certify teachers, and actually pay the entire teacher corps salaries and benefits, which means that they bear more than 65% of the total cost of education, though they use national funds and tuition receipts to do it.

The real direction for school systems is provided by a network of statutorily authorized Education Commissions, which are bodies of from three to five ordinary citizens appointed by either a governor or a mayor, with the consent of the relevant Assembly. In addition, members appointed in municipalities must be approved by the Education Commission of the prefecture, and those appointed at the prefectural level are approved by the MESC. Those commissioners serve four-year staggered terms and are either non-political, or there must be no majority of members of the commission from a single political party. All prefectures and 3,440 municipalities have appointed such commissions. Their major responsibilities are as follows:

1. Appoint and dismiss school superintendents.
2. Establish schools, libraries, and museums.
3. Approve and revise curricula within the Course of Study approved by the MESC.
4. Appoint and dismiss teachers.
5. Purchase textbooks and other instructional materials.
6. Establish and finance school lunch programs.
7. Establish social education programs.
8. Provide for the training of teachers.

The chairs of these commissions are appointed by the local chief executive, and they are nominally responsible to them, but in fact most commissions operate with a good deal of independence, especially in matters of professional educational judgement. The chief executive does play an important role in education to the extent that he compiles and executes the school system budget, as part of the overall budget for the municipality. In addition, he collects school fees and charges which become offsetting revenues in the budget. Other parts of the city administration may support the school system in service capacities such as the actual construction of school buildings, and disposal of obsolete buildings, and some supply and transportation support.

The budget process links to certain standards established for school operation. For example, the budget, which goes all the way to the MESC for final approval, is formulated on the basis of certain computed standards, such as that there will be no fewer than twelve, and no more than 18 classes offered in any elementary school; or that the average number of pupils in any elementary school class will be between 40 and 45. Funds are then computed based on these standards and not on actual facts. In reality, only 20% of the elementary schools meet the standard for number of classes, with 33% exceeding 18, and 46% having fewer than twelve students. Also, the average number of students in class is about 34, and only 25% of classes really meet the standard. While the MESC is very reluctant to pressure schools to "correct" the degree of compliance with these standards, the use of the standards tends to understate actual need, reduce the proportion of national funds for the system, and leave either the prefecture of the municipality holding the bag for the difference.

There are, however, two special programs for which the national government has more or less gotten stuck with the check. The first is the school lunch program, which started as a social welfare program in 1954, but somewhere along the line has become an entitlement. It is estimated that almost 99% of all elementary school students now receive a free school lunch, and the national government subsidizes all aspects of the program, including its administrative costs.

The student aid program is more narrow, but has high public acceptance and probably does the image of the MESC a lot of good. The program provides aid to needy families each month for students in the compulsory grades. It covers expenses such as special transportation to and from school, school supplies, children's clothing, rain boots and umbrellas, and school satchels. In 1983, about 1,040,000 students, or 6% of the total of 17.5 million in the compulsory grades received one or more elements of this assistance.

THE POLITICS OF EDUCATION

Any public program in Japan as well as in other countries, must be played out as part of the overall political and public policy system, but the Japanese have had special kinds of political problems. About 60% of school teachers belong to one or more of six unions. The Japan Teachers' Union is the largest, with an estimated membership (1982) of just under 600,000. These unions have the right by law to organize and to negotiate with local school and government authorities concerning working conditions and administrative actions which will have significant effect on teacher status. This does not include the right of general collective bargaining, especially with respect to compensation, nor does it include the right to strike.

Unfortunately, the Japan Teachers' Union and the much smaller leftist Japan Senior High School Teachers' Union, have become bastions of socialist activity and are highly political in character. In almost every year there are publicity campaigns and actual or threatened strikes and "job actions" which go far beyond legitimate concerns about working conditions and are essentially adversarial political activities. The national government is always a conservative government, and the majority of local governments are too and, therefore, these disputes take on the character of clashes of socialist vs. conservative political philosophy. Unions are active players in political campaigns, and constantly seek to build networks of supporters among local political figures, members of education commissions, and socialist members of university faculties in support of their political activities.

One of the facts of life which seems to explain much about the reticence of the MESC is that these unions are the implacable foes of any policy of action of the ministry. As Steven R. Reed puts it[5] "Consensus decision-making does not seem to work in education." Any boldness of action can be expected to meet with immediate and vigorous resistance and public conflict, making the politics of education a high risk, low profit venture. And once again, there are public employees put in the anomalous position of having two loyalties. They seem to remain loyal to their union, even when there are substantial indications that these unions, in the long run, are harmful to their profession.

Notes

1. The Fundamental Law of Education (1947), Article 1.
2. ibid, Article 3.
3. ibid, Article 6.
4. Reischauer, Edwin O., *The Japanese*, p. 175, Cambridge, Mass.: Harvard University Press, 1978.
5. Reed (1986: 118).

11 The Uses of Public Corporations and Public Enterprises

Part of the redesign of the institutional architecture of government which took place after World War II was the creation of a structure of government corporations at the national level and public enterprises at the local government level. This development was in part a recognition of the fact that the existing standard administrative structures were weak and needed rapid reinforcement, but there was also a deliberate sense that such standard bureaucracies were not necessarily the best instruments for the execution of certain public purposes where operational efficiency was a major concern. At the same time, few could predict the exceedingly rapid growth and enormous success of Japanese industry and commerce, and public corporations were seen as a necessary way for government to forge ahead in areas where the private sector, for various reasons, was not expected to develop adequately.

PUBLIC CORPORATIONS AT THE NATIONAL GOVERNMENT LEVEL

In 1946 there were 21 public corporations operating under the direction of the national government. In 1985 there were 102. There were successive waves in the growth and evolution of these organizations. In the period of 1946 to the mid-1950s, major direct government functions were "spun off" to create the Japanese National Railways, the Nippon Telegraph and Telephone Public Corporation, and the Japan Tobacco and Salt Public Corporation. In this same time period, a number of financing corporations were also created to channel loan funds to facilitate economic and industrial development, import–export growth, housing construction, and rapid modernization and expansion of basics like agriculture, forestry, and the fishing industry. Also, new special corporations were created through joint public–private financing. These included Japan Air Lines, the Electric Power Development Company, and the International Telephone and Telegraph Company.

In the succeeding ten-year period from 1955 to about the mid-1960s, public corporations were created for public infrastructure such as highways, airports, bridges, water and sewerage disposal systems, and hospitals. This was also the real period of growth of public corporations which were less "businesslike" in character but dealt with social programs, economic welfare, or research and scientific matters not yet ripe for commercial development. Corporations became the chosen organizational instrument for pollution control, nuclear research, space development, ship research, pension and welfare insurance administration, and the financing of social service needs in sanitation, medical care, consumer cooperatives, and even mutual aid associations for employees in various industries.

The proliferation of new corporations peaked in numbers by the late 1960s at 113. Since that time the policy of the Japanese government has been one of constraint and "no growth" in the public sector and this policy has included public corporations. In fact a special Commission for Administrative Reform in 1964 and a substantial reorganization program in 1979 both took the line that there needed to be a constraint exercised over the creative urge and a shake-out of existing corporations. Under the rubric of the "scrap and build" concept, several corporations were eliminated, consolidated, or reorganized. This same trend has been vigorously pursued as a result of the recommendations of the Nakasone Provisional Commission on Administrative Reform, including the sell-off of the Nippon Telegraph and Telephone Corporation, and the restructuring of the Japanese National Railways.

The commitment of the Japanese government to the extensive uses of public corporations has been very much driven by the sense that they contributed to managerial efficiency and productivity. The Japanese have thought more clearly than their American counterparts about the advantages and disadvantages in the uses of standard government agencies, public corporations, and the general private sector. There have been two common lines of reasoning behind the choice to create each public corporation:

1. To what extent does each program need to be controlled in order to implement public policy?
2. What is the maximum degree of management and operational flexibility and efficiency which can be achieved?

In making these choices, standard bureaucracies have been viewed as fully controllable in a policy sense, and effective in their own way, but not efficient mechanisms for conducting operations, especially those which are really competitive market-place operations. The private sector, on the other hand, was seen as the epitomy of operational effectiveness, but it was felt that private companies could not, and should not be tightly controlled as executors of public policy. Public corporations have proved to be a highly flexible middle course which has permitted the Japanese government to have some of the best of both worlds — responsiveness to policy and political direction, but also operational effectiveness.

When compared to national government ministries, public corporations have greater management independence and flexibility, particularly in organization, personnel matters, financial controls, and control over internal management systems and procedures. In some instances, such corporations are also given greater latitude in a policy sense, such as in the formulation of research policy in certain fields.

In comparison with the private sector, public corporations seem superior when the assurance of continuous, stable performance is necessary (a form of public utility concept), or where a strong public presence is needed to assure fairness and impartiality. Such public corporations have also been created where it is believed that the financial or technological risks were too high, or where prospects for reasonable profitability too low to expect the private sector to take the necessary initiative.

Control of Public Corporations

With far greater discipline than the American Congress, the Japanese Diet has adopted the approach that the presumed management advantages of public corporations need not result in any loss of political or policy direction. While US legislation chartering public corporations is vague and uncertain and follows no discernible pattern, the Japanese have laid down a base of common control elements for corporations which leaves no doubt as to how the public will is brought to bear.

Corporations are created by law, and each statute not only defines the powers which the corporation may exercise, but also the methods of supervision which the government will exercise. Each corporation is placed under the supervision of a relevant central government ministry which wields substantial power over it. Each corporation must prepare a business plan, a budget, and a financial plan which are all reviewed by the supervisory ministry. The Japanese rhetoric tends to describe these relationships in polite, cooperative terms, but bureaucratic instinct suggests that these reviews have the force of direction where necessary.

Of equal importance, ministers have the power to appoint or at least concur in the appointment of the top leadership of the corporation, and to set standards for executive compensation. Staffing plans are required and must be approved, and major internal management systems and processes cleared.

Financial oversight is equally stringent. In addition to ministerial approval of budget and financial plans, a corporation must obtain approval for any issuance of bonds, and for at least the general policy for charges, rates, or fees it will impose in its business operations. Where profits are generated, they may be placed back into business operations or accumulated in several types of reserve accounts. But surplus profits beyond these needs are subject to being paid over to the government, or may generate a decision to lower income until the revenue surplus is reduced.

In exchange for this oversight, public corporations are given great advantages. They have what amounts to a national charter in their enabling statute. Most have exclusive rights to their arena of business. They are fully financed by the national government, and may enjoy preferential loans, loan guarantees, or advantageous borrowing privileges when they are authorized to issue bonds. Once their budgets, business plans, and financial plans are approved, they enjoy relative freedom of operations. They usually have the authority to own and manage their own land, buildings, and equipment and may be authorized to exercise land condemnation authority and to enforce the collection of debt.

By these means, the central government is assured of having enough "handles" on its public corporations to assure their policy conformance. No doubt there is a good deal of tension between any given corporation and its supervisory ministry, but the impression gained is that ministries are willing to keep out of the internal management of the corporations. Ministry officials are undoubtedly tempted to impose their own judgement on corporations, but the effect of doing so would be to defeat the very reasons for their creation in the first place.

Problems with Public Corporations

Almost all of these corporate creations have come into existence since World War II, and many are less than 20 years old. Most were born in the period of great economic expansion and institutional creativity which ran from 1945 to the mid-1960s, and were carried along by the unparalleled economic success and public enthusiasm which marked this period. The constraints which began in the 1960s were not necessarily because of disenchantment with the public corporate form, but were part of a general "hold up and regroup" philosophy which began at that time.

The major Provisional Commission on Administrative Reform, which was initiated by Prime Minister Susuki in 1979 and vigorously continued by Prime Minister Nakasone, includes public corporations in its reform recommendations. In fact, it is widely felt that a publicly supported and highly visible reform program has given the Prime Minister the leverage to take on corporations like the Japanese National Railways, which is clearly a sacred cow having its own political wheelbase.

The Japanese National Railways illustrates one of the prime political and managerial problems represented by public corporations. Each corporation is a legal and policy commitment of the government, and most are totally financed by the government. What happens, therefore, when a corporation runs a deficit? In the short run, such devices as reserves, new bond issues, adjustments of charges and fees, or management stringencies may solve the problem, or mitigate the pain. But ultimately the government must pay and, in the case of the JNR, it has been paying at various levels of deficit since 1964. This has been the genesis of several waves of pressure on JNR to reduce its workforce and to divest itself of certain unprofitable branch lines. The 1979 reorganization mandated a decrease in JNR workforce from about 420,000 to a level of about 350,000 in an effort to cut losses which are close to one trillion yen annually.

But JNR also illustrates another major issue. When many of these corporations were created, it was in recognition that the private sector, for various reasons, was not ready or able to perform some function. But these perceptions may now be obsolete. While JNR struggles with its trillion yen deficit, other private Japanese railroads are operating profitably. This recognition led the reform commission to recommend to Prime Minister Nakasone in 1984 that the JNR be broken up into seven regional groupings, and sold off to the private sector within five years. This proposal has been accepted, and is being implemented as quickly as possible.

In a similar vein, a decision has been made to reorganize the Nippon Telegraph and Telephone Public Corporation into a private entity, with a central corporation operating long lines, and a series of local corporations offering local telephone services, in a pattern similar to the break-up of American Telephone and Telegraph in the United States. For the time being, the new corporation's stock will be held by the government, but the intent is that they will eventually be offered to the public when the market conditions are considered suitable. Similarly, the stock of the new local companies will be held by the central corporation, but will be sold publicly so that the local companies become fully independent.

The reform commission has also concluded that an additional 71 out of the initial total of 102 public corporations are likely candidates for privatization. Because of changes in social and economic perceptions, the whole standard of comparison for public corporations appears to have changed. In the past, when the basis of comparison for operational efficiency has been with government, public corporations have looked good. But the enormous success of Japanese industry, and the great pride which the Japanese people take in this success, is now making the private sector the standard of comparison, for drive, innovation, and cost-effectiveness. Against that standard, corporations are not nearly as attractive.

PUBLIC ENTERPRISES AT THE LOCAL GOVERNMENT LEVEL

In Japanese usage "local government" and "local public entity" are phrases which describe both the framework of regional prefectures and the range of cities, towns, and villages which are generically called municipalities. These local governments in turn are all legally entitled to create public enterprises and manage them either singly or jointly.

These public enterprises are not "corporations" in the sense that they are private organizations chartered under civil laws. They are creatures of the state, created by a government charter emanating usually from a legislative body, and they are clearly under the direction and control of the chief executives of local governments.

The growth of local governments in the post-war era included deliberate use of public enterprises, under a fairly uniform set of groundrules defined by national law. The basic intent of the local autonomy movement was to create a viable structure of prefectural and municipal governments capable of effectively administering what was expected to be a swiftly broadening range of domestic public services. As part of this movement, there were strong motivations for management effectiveness, which helps to explain the rapid growth of public enterprises. Japanese law created a clear legal authority to create public enterprises (and in some cases, public corporations) as alternatives to the use of standard civil service bureaucracies, and then sought to force, or at least encourage, the selection of the best form of organization to carry out public activities based almost entirely on judgements about how "businesslike" each activity was, and how management efficiency could best be achieved.

The Uses of Public Enterprises

There are 3,302 general-purpose local governments in Japan — 47 prefectures and 3,255 municipalities. All 47 of the prefectures and 98% of the municipalities, excluding only the smallest, are currently operating one or more public enterprises. Virtually all services to the public in commercial and residential water supply and sewerage are provided by such locally managed enterprises. In areas where private sector presence is stronger, the percentage is far smaller — 15% of hospital beds, 17% of local rail services, and 25% of local bus operations. Public enterprises are also used for generation of electricity and gas, home site preparation, harbor improvement, industrial water supply, and even for the operation of markets, wineries, race tracks and ski resorts. The public enterprise workforce of about 355,000 people is about 10% of the total workforce at the local government level.

As part of that exceptional series of statutes enacted by the Japanese Diet in the period 1945–55, which laid down the statutory basis for local autonomy, the Local Public Enterprise Law was passed in 1952, which formed the basis for the deployment of local public enterprises. It was felt that a national law was needed in order to make clear the authority of local public entities to create such corporations, as opposed to permitting such decisions to be made haphazardly and piecemeal by 3,300 jurisdictions. The law also imposes uniform groundrules for the operation of such enterprises, rather than leaving this definitional process to local option. Finally, the statute deals primarily with management stipulations — criteria on organization structure, finance, personnel, auditing, appointment authority, and major business practices. The law makes it clear that no public enterprise is in business for itself and each must be accountable to, and given direction by, the executive officers of the local government which creates it. Uniform basic principles were defined for them:

1. Each is expected to cover its costs from its revenues derived from fees or charges for its services. Where this is not possible or desirable (hospital service in rural areas, for example), the exact nature and extent of digression, and the sources and amounts of public subsidy are carefully defined and negotiated.
2. It must be understood that each remains a **public** enterprise, and that its fees or services must be fair and reasonable as judged by publicly debated standards for service levels and costs to the public. In other words, public enterprises cannot simply charge what the traffic will bear, or neglect marginal customer demands because they are not profitable, or even charge full cost recovery if the resultant public fees are seen as unreasonable. This has often led to needs for public subsidy, but that is acceptable.

The people who are expected to pass final judgement on how public enterprises satisfy these general principles are the political leadership of the local governments. Each is created either by a prefectural or municipal legislative body, or by a chief executive with legislative concurrence. Each public enterprise must have a single full-time general manager, and that person is appointed for a four-year term (reappointable) and removed by the chief executive of the local government. The manager of each public enterprise must prepare business plans, financial plans, personnel plans, schedules of intended fees or charges, and plans for bonds or loans. All of these plans are reviewed by the mayor or governor, and most must be explained and justified before assemblies. Where there are financial subsidies from the national government, or where some declared national objective or policy is involved, there are further approvals which must be obtained at the national level.

This is a very high degree of control not often paralleled in US experience. It is based on the concept that public enterprises cannot be permitted to define for themselves what the public interest is, nor can they be permitted to fail the test of public accountability to the political leadership. In fact, the only real advantage which exists between these enterprises and regular agencies lies in the management flexibilities which they are given. Once the managers have received buy-offs of their plans they are relatively free to manage the enterprise — to define service, hire and fire the workforce, let contracts, shift prices, and acquire and dispose of assets. Salary and allowances for employees are set by by-law, and tend to conform to civil service norms, but are free to differ, if necessary, to take advantage of the market-place. Local government civil service wage scales are relatively high, and wage latitude is an important element of the public enterprise advantage. Employees are permitted to organize and to engage in somewhat constrained collective bargaining, but are not given the right to strike.

ARE PUBLIC ENTERPRISES REALLY PRODUCTIVE?

Productivity or management effectiveness are not easily definable concepts in the public sector, and they are certainly not limited to internal management issues or how hard people work. The Japanese have always insisted that public enterprises must respond to public policy, and there are many elements of these public policies which run counter to maximum "efficiency" in pure operational terms.

Most of the major areas of public enterprise — hospitals, transportation, water supply, sewerage — are now plagued with serious management problems and growing deficits between income and expenses. Many of these problems stem from shifts in general economic conditions, where the capability or willingness to finance expansion of public services is relatively less. It also appears that the Japanese have often been no more skilled in predicting the future than the rest of the world. Much planning for construction and increases in service levels was based on presumed perpetual increases in funding and demand, which are now seen as seriously unreal. In some areas this led to overbuilding; water supply systems, for example, are now operating at 58% of capacity. The energy crisis of the 1970s had a sobering effect on Japanese economic expectations which has radically changed general public attitudes, and the new conservatism has been percolating through the public sector.

In summary, public corporations and public enterprises are certainly not able to escape the pressures and problems of functioning in an increasingly tougher economic environment. On balance, however, the flexibility of the corporate or enterprise form has had real public value. One only needs to contemplate these same problems being confronted by some rigid bureaucracy to appreciate the advantages of managerial flexibility. On the other hand, the complexities and dysfunctions of the political arena, which are beyond the control of operating managers, are themselves the cause of many of the problems of these institutions. Some of the rhetoric about public enterprise performance reveals the same tendency found in the US to call for greater "management efficiency" instead of facing up to the real political or policy issues involved.

A couple of examples of the impact of the new economic reality on public enterprises may be of value.

Water Supply

Water supply services are a mandated local government monopoly and have been a top national priority for many years because of industrial and residential growth and rice cultivation. Substantial national government subsidies have been paid since 1956, but mostly for special needs such as the development of new water resources, and for dealing with land subsidence in areas of large underground pumping. Water supply facilities in total are profitable, but more than 22% of the public enterprises are in deficit situations and this includes many large city systems. Costs of new construction or replacement are now very high and lead times for construction have grown excessively. Political pressure is strong to hold down rates and to expand service into remaining marginal service areas.

At the same time the perception gained is that the management of water supply public enterprises has done well over the long haul, and that the flexibilities of the public enterprise structure have in fact proved their value. Service has been expanded to meet needs, and income from rates has largely kept up with expenses. While over-building is obvious, it is now possible to avoid some new costly construction, and to satisfy some of the demand for extension of service into marginal customer areas. Total bonded indebtedness is actually decreasing, and management is slowly retiring debt and substituting growing internal reserves as a means of cutting interest expense and providing funds for future construction. The capacity to use internal funding reserves and accrual accounts in itself justifies the value of the public enterprise model in this activity.

Transportation

Transportation public enterprises are in far greater trouble than water supply enterprises. They have had to cope with more drastic external shifts, but there is some indication that their management has coped less effectively.

Within the total transportation system in Japan, very drastic shifts have occurred in two decades, as shown in Table 11.1. This means that Japan has "enjoyed" the same overpowering shift toward the use of automobiles which the US has experienced, and with the same drastic consequences to other forms of mass transportation. Total ridership by other than the automobile has been essentially a zero sum situation. Street cars have been deliberately eliminated because of their interference with auto street traffic, but those riders shifted to buses; then some bus riders shifted to subways, but throughout there has been a steady drain-off of transit and train riders to automobiles.

This shift has pushed large segments of the transportation system into deficit situations in which they are more reliant than ever on governmental subsidy. But this has also meant growing conflict between public policies and political yearnings for more and better service, and the growing recognition that the basic public enterprise concept of self-sufficiency is perhaps no longer realistic.

Both the political leadership and the managers of public enterprises are attempting to cope with these deficit operations. National policy has turned conservative about further construction of expensive subway routes, just as it has in the Reagan administration.

Table 11.1:   Total Passenger Carriage (%)

	1960	*1981*
Buses	31%	19%
JNR	25%	13%
Private railroads	23%	15%
Street cars	10%	--
Subways	2%	7%
Automobiles	8%	46%
Domestic air travel	--	.1%

The pattern of deployment of national government subsidies which is capable of considerable fine-tuning, has been shifted toward productivity and cost-saving initiatives, including phase-out of old two-operator buses, more bus route consolidations, and encouragement of private sector companies. The national government has also shown a willingness to help clean up some of the large bonded indebtedness, and to forestall a growth in bad debt situations by special financial subsidies which absorb part of debt interest costs, help retire debt principal, or even redeem more expensive bond issues.

Over and above these broader policy and financial changes, however, there is a parallel concern that public enterprise leadership has not performed well in its internal management, and the presumed advantages of the public enterprise approach have not been fully realized. Since there are private sector companies in the transportation field, direct comparisons with the private sector are possible. Public enterprises are said to have staffs which are 10% larger for comparable services and which receive wages which are about 25% higher. Fares are higher and profit on services are 50% greater than their private sector counterparts. Public enterprises tend to usurp most of the more dense and profitable travel corridors, although this means that they suffer slowing of service from congestion. In sum, a case can be made that the public enterprise model is far less successful in this arena and looks more like an inflexible bureaucracy than hoped or expected.

12 The Culture of the Civil Service

The Japanese seem to agree that politics are the link between the will of the people and the objectives and designs of public programs. But there also appears to be a greater acceptance than in the United States that the administration of public programs is very important and that there should be a strong and effective career civil service to carry out that work. In other words, the Japanese are less inclined to believe that good public programs stop at the point of political decision-making, or that politicians are the best people to manage public services.

Thus, the Japanese are strongly behind the concept of a career civil service which conforms to the ethics of public service as it has evolved in western nations — that is, a strong sense of public service, a striving to make balanced judgements in the public interest, and a commitment to do productive and efficient work on the public's behalf.

But this is a commitment which has been in place only since the creation of the new Constitution, and it has been grafted onto an older structure and philosophy about government which was in many ways directly the opposite. This can best be illustrated by looking at the older style of local government. The centralist philosophy of government which prevailed in Japan from the Meiji Restoration until the post-World War II era had a high cost in terms of the neglect of local governments and their workforces. Most communities were ill prepared to take advantage of the new Constitution of 1945 which triggered the redesign of their structures and the redefinition of their personnel systems.

Most communities had a long "tradition" of almost feudal control of public workers who were mainly blue collar workers, laborers, construction workers, and a few skilled and semi-skilled craftsmen. Most were ill trained and often ignorant and uneducated. There was an absence of skilled specialists educated and trained in administrative capabilities, and of trained technicians and professionals. Many employees were part-time or casual workers who were hired and released under vaguely defined staff "allotments" and unexplained work rules. Cronyism was rampant and there was little or no thought given to building a stable, competent career workforce.

Such systems are highly inequitable. Some classes of officials were elite and superior, while whole groups of employees were kept in auxiliary situations and never reached anything like a permanent status. Many of the top positions were filled (as they are today) by officials assigned by the central government. While most of these officials were honest and competent, they represented an elite which saw themselves as servants of the Emperor and certainly not servants of the people. Their presence was often resented because they represented the imposition of central authority. They also encumbered attractive jobs which were thus not available to ambitious local aspirants. Their own careers were linked to the national government, and that often made them indifferent to longer-term local needs. In general, the situation was far better in the national government, which was prestigious if undemocratic, and it was better in prefectural governments or in large municipalities than in rural areas and small towns.

The national consensus about government which evolved swiftly after the war wisely recognized that this weak and haphazard system was hopelessly inadequate. The nation's commitment to industrialization and its broader and more humanitarian social agenda were correctly understood to create a collateral demand for a far more skilled and educated body of public servants to create and manage more technically advanced public services.

The new Constitution became the basis for the promulgation of a series of watershed national laws which imposed national standards and groundrules on local governments, but permitted them to become more stable and professional. The principal statutes were the Local Autonomy Law which created the framework for local governments and defined the general structure for public administration; and the Local Public Service Law of 1950 which imposed a single uniform personnel system for both prefectures and municipalities, replacing inconsistent and ill defined local systems. This law closely paralleled the National Public Service Law, which did the same thing for employees of the national government in 1947. All public employees were clearly stated to be servants of the whole community, and it was equally clear that the designation was intended to be a position of honor and prestige. The public is asked to respect their public servants and accord them a reasonable status in the community. Public employees in return are asked to serve their community honestly and well and work hard for the public good.

The Local Public Service Law lays down a complete personnel management system which is to be democratic, equitable, and efficient. It established groundrules for key personnel functions such as selection, appointment, position management, working conditions, status, promotion, discipline, training, work performance evaluation, and the protection of employee benefits and welfare. In addition, it exempted local public service employees from many of the national laws dealing with labor relations, and created a special labor relations environment for the public service which permits employees to organize and to bargain (both denied to national government employees), but not the right to strike.

Special public service laws were passed for specific classes of local public employees, notably those in education, law enforcement, fire protection, routine labor, and public enterprises. Special treatment is given to political officers such as mayors or members of prefectural or municipal legislative bodies, and for special bodies such as inspection commissions, election agencies, and for commissions supervising education, public safety, and the personnel system itself.

Behind all of these statutes is the concept of a merit system free from political intervention, and the concept of equity and equality with respect to race, sex, social status, religious belief, family status, and political conviction. This is basically a "right to work" system, modified by the overall status as servants of the community, which means that reductions in employment or wages can be imposed if necessary to meet changes in community needs.

Employment levels of the public service workforce expanded rapidly in the post-war period. Employment peaked in the national government in 1965, but not until about 1982 in local governments. Table 12.1 shows these trends for various elements of local government. While this increase was necessary, it produced the same kind of counter-reaction which "capped" the national public workforce and contributed to the initiation of the Provisional Commission Administrative Reform and other efforts to press for holding the line on local government employment.

During this entire period, the national government was increasingly worried about the growth of government and this was especially true after 1975, when it began deficit financing and anti-cyclical economic measures on a large scale. The national government increasingly used its "administrative guidance" and the network of its budget/allocation financial control mechanisms to press local governments toward more stringent staff control and productivity improvement. While no hard targets for work-

Table 12.1:   Local Government Personnel
(permanent, full-time; in thousands)

	1968	1973	1979	1982
Regular government service	820	1004	1135	1155
Prefectures	(322)	(362)	(338)	(334)
Municipalities	(498)	(642)	(797)	(821)
Education	972	1076	1241	1303
Teachers	(766)	(828)	(946)	(993)
Others	(141)	(248)	(296)	(310)
Police	184	214	237	244
Fire defense	58	90	118	126
Public enterprises	301	344	377	388
Total	2335	2728	3108	3216

force levels are set as the Cabinet does for the national government, local governments are now endlessly being urged to hold the line in all areas. Exceptions are made only where there is a specific national policy imperative which is being implemented, as, for example, a planned growth in university-level technical education, or the badly needed extension of sewerage trcatment capacity.

THE CULTURE OF THE SENIOR CIVIL SERVICE

The higher levels of the career civil service have always been seen as an elite, but, starting with the new Constitution in 1945, the nature of the elite changed dramatically and for the better. In just the last decade there are new tides beginning to flow to broaden the base for these senior people without sacrificing their perceived quality. In the national government, the civil service has eight grades. The top three are generally regarded as the senior level of the service, and there are approximately 16,000 positions in these grades. Entry into these positions is ostensibly by a series of merit examinations, but this doesn't begin to convey the real sense of the process and why it remains Jan elitist system. There are said to be between 500 and 600 really first-rate positions in the national government which are the prime targets for an intense competition which begins in the universities. For many years, the prime source of intake into the government has been the Law School at the University of Tokyo, and in the 1930s more than 90% of all of the people who rose to senior positions in the national government were from that school. While that number has decreased, it still remains in the range of 50%. The curriculum there was not strictly law, but a specially prepared program in public law, regulation, and public administration. Entry examinations into the national public service were staggeringly difficult tests dealing with a mass of legal and technical detail, drawn directly from the Tokyo University Law School program, and often marked by its faculty.

In recent years, there has been a concerted effort, led by the National Personnel Authority, to break this incestuous system, first to open up opportunities for graduates of other universities; second to rely less on set examinations which measure only the ultimate grasp of nitty gritty, and to begin to rely on measures or judgements of total ability; and third to open up the system, slowly and reluctantly, to women.

But the Japanese civil service, like the British aristocracy, is the ultimate "old boy network", and the literature from academics and practitioners in public administration continues to bemoan the painfully slow rate of change. Why this is so can be better understood by looking at how the internal machinery of ministries really operates.

Each year a new "class" of professional-level employees of the highest credentials is taken into the public service, and more than 50% still comes from the University of Tokyo Law School. This class sticks together and develops its own intense internal loyalties. As the years go by, each class competes with older classes and fends off younger ones. Over time, each class develops its "stars" who advance more rapidly than others. These stars become the leaders of their class and the class helps them to get into the best ministries (Finance, International Trade and Industry, Foreign Affairs, Economic Planning Agency), and the most sought-after positions. The leaders in turn help their classmates by promoting them, slipping them into influential second- and third-level positions, giving them good special assignments, and anything else for the good of the class. The very brightest stars of these class cliques point themselves toward the position of Permanent Deputy Minister, which is the pinnacle of the career service and in fact the real power base for the direction of both the policies and the administration of the affairs of the ministry.

But many of these leaders also phase over into the political world and join political "factions" which link together networks of supporters in the executive branch of government, the Diet, and the ruling Liberal Democratic Party. There is a tradition of senior civil servants running for office, and in recent years about 25% of the lower House of Representatives, and as many as 35% of the House of Councillors are former civil servants. Most Prime Ministers in the post-war period have served such apprenticeships in the civil service.

Finally, the very best of the careerists are ultimately selected for the positions of Permanent Deputy Minister in the twelve ministries and in a few other key jobs. As these winners on the long competition are selected, their rivals will often retire from the field — literally. But they are not "losers" because they move into the very top-level positions in the private sector, where they are highly sought. Others may move to trade associations, university faculties, or into the private practice of law, but the "old boy network" never ceases to exist. This life-long pattern of friendship and alliance goes a long way to explain the exceptional rapport between the various leadership elements in Japanese society, and the high degree to which a common view is shared about government and political matters.

This structure and internal "culture" is very different than that found in the United States national government where the line of demarcation between political officials and senior career officers is sharply drawn and stringently enforced. The US President is authorized to appoint perhaps 4,500 "political appointees" to support his administration. When a President from the other party is elected, all but a handful of the incumbents in these positions are immediately removed and new loyalists appointed. The crucial point, however, is that, unlike the Japanese structure, these political positions are almost all of the top policy and management positions in the departments and agencies, and even the senior career executives are kept down in the second- and third-level positions, which are often technical and expert positions rather than policy or decision-making. Top civil servants are deliberately kept out of political meetings and negotiations, and they rarely participate except as technical experts in testimony or political negotiations with the Congress, or in the political horse-trading with powerful client and constituent groups.

There are many concerns about the Japanese system which are reflected by both scholars and practitioners. There is the desire to see the system loosened up to provide more opportunity for graduates of other universities and for talents other than master legal technicians. The "old boy network" seems to be waning under the pressure of a more diverse and more sophisticated government, where policy formulation is more complex and requires more effort to build public consensus by broad consideration of the issues. Finally, the leveling of the economy and the subsequent era of deficit financing of governments has shaken the previous conviction that the decisions of the new elite are always right. But the important fact remains that government service does bring in a substantial number of the very best people in Japanese society, and it does train them and equip them with the kind of broad experience and ability to be leaders which has proved to be of great value to the country.

TRENDS IN LOCAL GOVERNMENT ADMINISTRATIVE REFORM[1]

Japanese local governments have not escaped many of the bureaucratic attitudes which can be found in public organizations all over the world. But both national and local officials are expressing real belief that these attitudes are beginning to change for the better. Time after time, the most compelling leverage which is producing this change is the growing tendency to compare public sector performance to that of Japan's exciting and highly successful private sector. Invidious comments by corporate officers speak of the "paradise of public office", referring to their presumed slow pace, risk-free environment, and relatively high wages. The public more frequently and publicly ask "Why can't our government agencies be more like our marvelous corporations?". Table 12.2 shows the results of a recent questionnaire revealing much about public vs. private employee attitudes.

Table 12.2:   Employee Opinion Survey

Key Opinions	*Public*	*Private*
Promotion/pay not performance determined	57%	21%
Not much need to consider cost (profit)	36	6
Seniority is important	43	21
Behaviour more important than performance	44	22
Can't make full use of my talents	25	10
Factions and personal considerations prevail	37	16
Work monotonous and inactive	30	14
Want higher position	36	70

Source A Comparative Study of Public and Private Organizations pp. 15–43. Kato, Tomide, *Local Government Review In Japan*, No. 9 1981, edited by the Local Government Research and Data Center, Tokyo, Japan.

Old standards of behavior have tended to be authoritative and not competitive. Public employees believe that they can't buck the political leadership which wants loyalty, blind obedience, and respect for authority ("the will of the boss is the will of the people"), rather than internal entrepreneurship or "struggle".

The new attitudes of both public managers and employees seem to center in part around management effectiveness and in part around personal development. Personnel systems are changing to place less emphasis on the "right" college degree, seniority, and the use of written examinations. More emphasis is now placed on practical job performance, evaluation of potential, and qualities of leadership and initiative.

Employee training and development is increasingly seen as a reward for top performance and generates high motivation, especially among younger professionals. More prefectures and municipalities now have their own training institutes, or send employees to national colleges or outside schooling. The Ministry of Home Affairs maintains a Local Autonomy College which trains local government executives and elected officials. Employee mobility assignments, rotational projects, or on-the-job training are growing in popularity. For richer communities programs of work or study assignments in other countries are possible and are wildly popular and coveted.

In interviews with public officials there was one technique which was cited by every one of them. All pointed to the great value of a style of "group consciousness" in all offices. They all spoke of the value of the "mass ability" of each employee group to function as a team — each member working together on the total work require- ment, as opposed to the efforts of individuals working on narrow specialist jobs which don't integrate well into total performance. Many of these officials also contrasted this to what they perceive to be the American government model which relies on narrow rigid job descriptions that frustrate team performance and individual co- operative attitudes.

Japanese public unions are universally cited as the most negative force which stultifies both managerial reform and personnel change. Both national and local government officials obviously regard unions with fear and loathing. The principal labor federations of local public service personnel are the All-Japan Prefectural and Municipal Workers' Union, the Japan Federation of Urban Transportation Workers' Union, and the National Water Supply Workers' Union. The transport and water supply unions deal with employees of public enterprises, as does much of the prefectural/municipal union. In total, these unions represent about 1,363,000 employees (including 125,400 in public enterprises), or about 79.4% of all local public employees.

Despite the fact that these unions are forbidden by law from striking, there has been a persistent pattern of such strikes or work stoppages, involving as many as 550,000 workers at a time. In 1981 a total of 3,320,000 person-days of work were lost due to strikes. Such strikes have dealt with wages, pension and welfare systems, and opposition to reductions in retirement benefits; but they have also dealt with resistance to needed reforms in the personnel system and general resistance to the program of administrative reform pushed by Prime Minister Nakasone and his predecessor.

One of the interesting customs of Japanese labor is the "spring offensive" — a united labor strike program involving both public and private unions which occurs in many years as leverage on upcoming labor negotiations. In 1982, however, only the three local government public unions actually struck, while private sector unions and even the national public employee unions settled negotiations without lost labor hours. Notwithstanding the illegality of public employee strikes, these local labor organizations are now widely seen as more militant and more intractable than their private sector counterparts.

In private sector organizations, the sense of external (and international) competition and the sense of close identification by workers with the fate of the company seem to produce a banding together of workers and managers which contributes to the strength of the organization. Corporate workers do not resist change or automation because they believe that they will be taken care of and will benefit from any improvement in the company's success. This is seen as one of the keystones to the high productivity of these corporations.

In the public sector, however, the "union vs. management" attitude frustrates this process, and workers are caught between a natural ethic to cooperate and serve the community, and a loyalty to the union. Resolution of this kind of conflict appears to be the one major area of public management with which Japanese public administration seems unable to cope successfully.

Note

1. Much of the material in this section was obtained by the author in interviews with officials of the National Personnel Authority, and with local government officials in Tokyo, Kyoto, Hiroshima city and prefecture, and Mitaka City.

Appendix

THE CONSTITUTION OF JAPAN

We, the Japanese people, acting through our duly elected representatives in the National Diet, determined that we shall secure for ourselves and our posterity the fruits of peaceful cooperation with all nations and the blessings of liberty throughout this land, and resolved that never again shall we be visited with the horrors of war through the action of government, do proclaim that sovereign power resides with the people and do firmly establish this Constitution. Government is a sacred trust of the people, the authority for which is derived from the people, the powers of which are exercised by the representatives of the people, and the benefits of which are enjoyed by the people. This is a universal principle of mankind upon which this Constitution is founded. We reject and revoke all constitutions, laws, ordinances, and rescripts in conflict herewith.

We, the Japanese people, desire peace for all time and are deeply conscious of the high ideals controlling human relationships, and we have determined to preserve our security and existence trusting in the justice and faith of the peace-loving peoples of the world. We desire to occupy an honored place in an international society striving for the preservation of peace and the banishment of tyranny and slavery, oppression and intolerance for all time from the earth. We recognize that all peoples of the world have the right to live in peace, free from fear and want.

We believe that no nation is responsible to itself alone, but the laws of political morality are universal; and that obedience to such laws is incumbent upon all nations who would sustain their own sovereignty and justify the sovereign relationships with other nations.

We, the Japanese people, pledge our national honor to accomplish these high ideals and purpose with all our resources.

CHAPTER I: THE EMPEROR

Article 1. The Emperor shall be the symbol of the State and of the unity of the people, deriving his position from the will of the people with whom resides sovereign power.

Article 2. The Imperial Throne shall be dynastic and succeeded to in accordance with the Imperial House Law passed by the Diet.

Article 3. The advice and approval of the Cabinet shall be required for all acts of the Emperor in matters of state, and the Cabinet shall be responsible therefor.

Article 4. The Emperor shall perform only such acts in matters of state as are provided for in this Constitution and he shall not have powers related to government.

The Emperor may delegate the performance of his acts in matters of state as may be provided by law.

Article 5. When, in accordance with the Imperial House Law, a Regency is established, the Regent shall perform his acts in matters of state in the Emperor's name. In this case, paragraph one of the preceding article will be applicable.

Article 6. The Emperor shall appoint the Prime Minister as designated by the Diet. The Emperor shall appoint the Chief Judge of the Supreme Court as designated by the Cabinet.

Article 7. The Emperor, with the advice and approval of the Cabinet, shall perform the following acts in matters of state on behalf of the people:

> Promulgation of amendments of the Constitution, laws, cabinet orders, and treaties.
> Convocation of the Diet.
> Dissolution of the House of Representatives.
> Proclamation of the general election of members of the Diet.
> Attestation of the appointment and dismissal of Ministers of State and other officials as provided for by law, and of full powers and credentials of ambassadors and ministers.
> Attestation of general and special amnesty, commutation of punishment, reprieve, and restoration of rights.
> Awarding honors.
> Attestation of instruments of ratification and other diplomatic documents as provided for by law.
> Receiving foreign ambassadors and ministers.
> Performance of ceremonial functions.

Article 8. No property can be given to, or received by, the Imperial House, nor can any gifts be made therefrom, without authorization of the Diet.

CHAPTER II: RENUNCIATION OF WAR

Article 9. Aspiring sincerely to an international peace based on justice and order, the Japanese people forever renounce war as a sovereign right of the nation and the threat or use of force as a means of settling international disputes.

In order to accomplish the aim of the preceding paragraph, land, sea, and air forces, as well as other war potential, will never be maintained. The right of belligerency of the state will not be recognized.

CHAPTER III: RIGHTS AND DUTIES OF THE PEOPLE

Article 10. The conditions necessary for being a Japanese national shall be determined by law.

Article 11. The people shall not be prevented from enjoying any of the fundamental human rights. Those fundamental human rights guaranteed to the people by this Constitution shall be conferred upon the people of this land and future generations as eternal and inviolate rights.

Article 12. The freedoms and rights guaranteed to the people by this Constitution shall be maintained by the constant endeavor of the people, who shall refrain from any abuse of these freedoms and rights and shall always be responsible for utilizing them for the public welfare.

Article 13. All of the people shall be respected as individuals. Their right to life, liberty, and the pursuit of happiness shall, to the extent that does not interfere with the public welfare, be the supreme consideration in legislation and in other governmental affairs.

Article 14. All of the people are equal under the law and there shall be no discrimination in political, economic or social relations because of race, creed, sex, social status or family origin.

Peers and peerage shall not be recognized.

No privilege shall accompany any award of honor, decoration or any distinction, nor shall any such award be valid beyond the lifetime of the individual who now holds or hereafter may receive it.

Article 15. The people have the inalienable right to choose their public officials and to dismiss them.

All public officials are servants of the whole community and not of any group thereof.

Universal adult suffrage is guaranteed with regard to the election of public officials.

In all elections, secrecy of the ballot shall not be violated. A voter shall not be answerable, publicly or privately, for the choice he has made.

Article 16. Every person shall have the right of peaceful petition for the enactment, repeal or amendment of the laws, ordinances or regulations and for other matters; nor shall any person be in any way discriminated against for sponsoring such a petition.

Article 17. Every person may sue for redress as provided for by law from the State or a public entity, in case he has suffered damage through the illegal act of any public official.

Article 18. No person shall be held in bondage of any kind. Involuntary servitude, except as punishment for crime, is prohibited.

Article 19. Freedom of thought and conscience shall not be violated.

Article 20. Freedom of religion is guaranteed to all. No religious organization shall receive any privileges from the State, or exercise any political authority.

Article 21. Freedom of assembly and association as well as speech, press and all other forms of expression are guaranteed.

No censorship shall be maintained, nor shall the secrecy of any means of communication be violated.

Article 22. Every person shall have freedom to choose and change his residence and to choose his occupation to the extent that it does not interfere with the public welfare.

Freedom of all persons to move to a foreign country and to divest themselves of their nationality shall be inviolate.

Article 23. Academic freedom is guaranteed.

Article 24. Marriage shall be based only on the mutual consent of both sexes and it shall be maintained through mutual cooperation with equal rights of husband and wife as a basis.

With regard to choice of spouse, property rights, inheritance, choice of domicile, divorce and other matters pertaining to marriage and the family, laws shall be enacted from the standpoint of individual dignity and the essential equality of the sexes.

Article 25. All people shall have the right to maintain the minimum standards of wholesome and cultured living.

In all spheres of life, the State shall use its endeavors for the promotion and extension of social welfare and security, and of public health.

Article 26. All people shall have the right to receive an equal education corresponding to their ability, as provided for by law.

All people shall be obligated to have all boys and girls under their protection receive ordinary education as provided by law. Such compulsory education shall be free.

Article 27. All people shall have the right and the obligation to work.

Standards for wages, hours, rest and other working conditions shall be fixed by law.

Children shall not be exploited.

Article 28. The right of workers to organize and to bargain and act collectively is guaranteed.

Article 29. The right to own or to hold property is inviolable.

Property rights shall be defined by law, in conformity with the public welfare.

Private property may be taken for public use upon just compensation therefor.

Article 30. The people shall be liable to taxation as provided by law.

Article 31. No person shall be deprived of life or liberty, nor shall any other criminal penalty be imposed, except according to procedures established by law.

Article 32. No person shall be denied the right of access to the courts.

Article 33. No person shall be apprehended except upon warrant issued by a competent judicial officer which specifies the offense being committed.

Article 34. No person shall be arrested or detained without being at once informed of the charges against him or without the immediate privilege of counsel; nor shall he be detained without adequate cause; and upon demand of any person such cause must be immediately shown in open court in his presence and the presence of his counsel.

Article 35. The right of all persons to be secure in their homes, papers and effects against entries, searches and seizures shall not be impaired except upon warrant issued for adequate cause and particularly describing the place to be searched and things be seized, or except as provided for by Article 33.

Each search or seizure shall be made upon separate warrant issued by a competent judicial officer.

Article 36. The infliction of torture by any public officer and cruel punishments are absolutely forbidden.

Article 37. In all criminal cases the accused shall enjoy the right to a speedy and public trial by an impartial tribunal.

He shall be permitted full opportunity to examine all witnesses, and he shall have the right of compulsory process for obtaining witnesses on his behalf at public expense.

At all times the accused shall have the assistance of competent counsel who shall, if the accused is unable to secure the same by his own efforts, be assigned to his use by the State.

Confession made under compulsion, torture or threat, or after prolonged arrest or detention shall not be admitted in evidence.

No person shall be convicted or punished in cases where the only proof against him is his own confession.

Article 38. No person shall be compelled to testify against himself.

Confession made under compulsion, torture or threat, or after prolonged arrest or detention shall not be admitted in evidence.

No person shall be convicted or punished in cases where the only proof against him is his own confession.

Article 39. No person shall be held criminally liable for an act which was lawful at the time it was committed, or of which he has been acquitted, nor shall he be placed in double jeopardy.

Article 40. Any person, in case he is acquitted after he has been arrested or detained, may sue the State for redress as provided by law.

CHAPTER IV: THE DIET

Article 41. The Diet shall be the highest organ of state power, and shall be the sole law-making organ of the State.

Article 42. The Diet shall consist of two Houses, namely the House of Representatives and the House of Councillors.

Article 43. Both Houses shall consist of elected members, representative of all the people.

The number of members of each House shall be fixed by law.

Article 44. The qualifications of members of both Houses and their electors shall be fixed by law. However, there shall be no discrimination because of race, creed, sex, social status, family origin, education, property or income.

Article 45. The term of office of members of the House of Representatives shall be four years. However, the term shall be terminated before the full term is up in case the House of Representatives is dissolved.

Article 46. The term of office of members of the House of Councillors shall be six years, and election for half the members shall take place every three years.

Article 47. Electoral districts, method of voting and other matters pertaining to the method of election of members of both Houses shall be fixed by law.

Article 48. No person shall be permitted to be a member of both Houses simultaneously.

Article 49. Members of both Houses shall receive appropriate annual payment from the national treasury in accordance with law.

Article 50. Except in cases provided by law, members of both Houses shall be exempt from apprehension while the Diet is in session, and any members apprehended before the opening of the session shall be freed during the term of the session upon demand of the House.

Article 51. Members of both Houses shall not be held liable outside the House for speeches, debates or votes cast inside the House.

Article 52. An ordinary session of the Diet shall be convened once per year.

Article 53. The Cabinet may determine to convene extraordinary sessions of the Diet. When a quarter or more of the total members of either House makes the demand, the Cabinet must determine on such convocation.

Article 54. When the House of Representatives is dissolved, there must be a general election of members of the House of Representatives within forty (40) days from the date of dissolution, and the Diet must be convened within thirty (30) days from the date of the election.

When the House of Representatives is dissolved, the House of Councillors is closed at the same time. However, the Cabinet may in time of national emergency convene the House of Councillors in emergency session.

Measures taken at such session as mentioned in the proviso of the preceding paragraph shall become null and void unless agreed to by the House of Representatives within a period of ten (10) days after the opening of the next session of the Diet.

Article 55. Each House shall judge disputes related to qualifications of its members. However, in order to deny a seat to any member it is necessary to pass a resolution by a majority of two-thirds or more of the members present.

Article 56. Business cannot be transacted in either House unless one-third or more of total membership is present.

All matters shall be decided, in each House, by a majority of those present, except as elsewhere provided in the Constitution, and in case of a tie, the presiding officer shall decide the issue.

Article 57. Deliberation in each House shall be public. However, a secret meeting may be held where a majority of two-thirds or more of those members present passes a resolution therefor.

Each House shall keep a record of proceedings. This record shall be published and given general circulation, excepting such parts of proceedings of secret sessions as may be deemed to require secrecy.

Upon demand of one-fifth or more of the members present, votes of the members on any matter shall be recorded in the minutes.

Article 58. Each House shall select its own president and other officials.

Each House shall establish its rules pertaining to meetings, proceedings and internal discipline, and may punish members for disorderly conduct. However, in order to expel a member, a majority of two-thirds or more of those members must pass a resolution thereon.

Article 59. A bill becomes a law on passage by both Houses, except as otherwise provided by the Constitution.

A bill which is passed by the House of Representatives, and upon which the House of Councillors makes a decision different from that of the House of Representatives, becomes law when passed a second time by the House of Representatives by a majority of two-thirds or more of the members present.

The provision of the preceding paragraph does not preclude the House of Representatives from calling for the meeting of a joint committee of both Houses, provided for by law.

Failure by the House of Councillors to take final action within sixty (60) days after receipt of a bill passed by the House of Representatives shall constitute a rejection of the said bill by the House of Councillors.

Article 60. The budget must first be submitted to the House of Representatives. Upon consideration of the budget, when the House of Councillors makes a decision different from that of the House of Representatives, and when no agreement can be reached even through a joint committee of both Houses, provided for by law, or in the case of failure by the House of Councillors to take final action within thirty (30) days, the period of recess excluded, after the receipt of the budget passed by the House of Representatives, the decision of the House of Representatives shall be the decision of the Diet.

Article 61. The second paragraph of the preceding article applies also to the Diet approval required for the conclusion of treaties.

Article 62. Each House may conduct investigations in relation to government, and may demand the presence and testimony of witnesses, and the production of records.

Article 63. The Prime Minister and other Ministers of State may, at any time, appear in either House for the purpose of speaking on bills, regardless of whether they are members of the House or not. They must appear when their presence is required in order to give answers or explanations.

Article 64. The Diet shall set up an impeachment court from among the members of both Houses for the purpose of trying those judges against whom removal proceedings have been instituted.

Matters relating to impeachment shall be provided by law.

CHAPTER V: THE CABINET

Article 65. Executive power shall be vested in the Cabinet.

Article 66. The Cabinet shall consist of the Prime Minister, who shall be its head, and other Ministers of State, as provided by law.

The Prime Minister and other Ministers of State must be civilians.

The Cabinet, in the exercise of executive power, shall be collectively responsible to the Diet.

Article 67. The Prime Minister shall be designated from among the members of the Diet by a resolution of the Diet. This designation shall precede all other business.

If the House of Representatives and the House of Councillors disagree and if no agreement can be reached even through a joint committee of both Houses, provided for by law, or the House of Councillors fails to make designation within ten (10) days, exclusive of the period of recess, after the House of Representatives has made designation, the decision of the House of Representatives shall be the decision of the Diet.

Article 68. The Prime Minister shall appoint the Ministers of State. However, a majority of their number must be chosen from among the members of the Diet.

The Prime Minister may remove the Ministers of State as he chooses.

Article 69. If the House of Representatives passes a non-confidence resolution, or rejects a confidence resolution, the Cabinet shall resign *en masse*, unless the House of Representatives in dissolved within ten (10) days.

Article 70. When there is a vacancy in the post of Prime Minister, or upon the first convocation of the Diet after a general election of members of the House of Representatives, the Cabinet shall resign *en masse*.

Article 71. In the cases mentioned in the two preceding articles, the Cabinet shall continue its function until the time when a new Prime Minister is appointed.

Article 72. The Prime Minister, representing the Cabinet, submits bills, reports on general national affairs and foreign relations to the Diet and exercises control and supervision over various administrative branches.

Article 73. The Cabinet, in addition to other general administrative functions, shall perform the following functions:

Administer the law faithfully; conduct affairs of state.

Manage foreign affairs.

Conclude treaties. However, it shall obtain prior or, depending on circumstances, subsequent approval of the Diet.

Administer the civil service, in accordance with standards established by law.

Prepare the budget, and present it to the Diet.

Enact Cabinet orders to execute the provisions of this Constitution and of the law. However, it cannot include penal provisions in such Cabinet orders unless authorized by such law.

Decide on general amnesty, special amnesty, commutation of punishment, reprieve, and restoration of rights.

Article 74. All laws and Cabinet orders shall be signed by the competent Minister of State and countersigned by the Prime Minister.

Article 75. The Ministers of State, during their tenure of office, shall not be subject to legal action without the consent of the Prime Minister. However, the right to take that action is not impaired hereby.

CHAPTER VI: JUDICIARY

Article 76. The whole judicial power is vested in a Supreme Court and in such inferior courts as are established by law.

No extraordinary tribunal shall be established, nor shall any organ or agency of the Executive be given final judicial power.

All judges shall be independent in the exercise of their conscience and shall be bound only by this Constitution and the laws.

Article 77. The Supreme Court is vested with the rule-making power under which it determines the rules of procedure and of practice, and of matters relating to attorneys, the internal discipline of the courts and the administration of judicial affairs.

Public procurators shall be subject to the rule-making power of the Supreme Court.

The Supreme Court may delegate the power to make rules for inferior courts to such courts.

Article 78. Judges shall not be removed except by public impeachment unless judicially declared mentally or physically incompetent to perform official duties. No disciplinary action against judges shall be administered by any executive organ or agency.

Article 79. The Supreme Court shall consist of a Chief Judge and such number of judges as may be determined by law; all such judges excepting the Chief Judge shall be appointed by the Cabinet.

The appointment of the judges of the Supreme Court shall be reviewed by the people at the first general election of members of the House of Representatives following their appointment, and shall be reviewed again at the first general election of members of the House of Representatives after a lapse of ten (10) years, and in the same manner thereafter.

In cases mentioned in the foregoing paragraph, when the majority of the votes favors the dismissal of a judge, he shall be dismissed.

Matters pertaining to review shall be prescribed by law.

The judges of the Supreme Court shall be retired upon the attainment of the age as fixed by law.

All such judges shall receive, at regular stated intervals, adequate compensation which shall not be decreased during their terms of office.

Article 80. The judges of the inferior courts shall be appointed by the Cabinet from a list of persons nominated by the Supreme Court. All such judges shall hold office for a term of ten (10) years with the privilege of reappointment, provided that they shall be retired upon the attainment of the ages as fixed by law.

The judges of the inferior courts shall receive, at regular stated intervals, adequate compensation which shall not be decreased during their terms of office.

Article 81. The Supreme Court is the court of last resort with power to determine the constitutionality of any law, order, regulation or official act.

Article 82. Trials shall be conducted and judgement declared publicly.

Where a court unanimously determines publicity to be dangerous to public order or morals, a trial may be conducted privately, but trials of political offenses, offenses involving the press or cases wherein the rights of people as guaranteed in Chapter III of this Constitution are in question shall always be conducted publicly.

CHAPTER VII: FINANCE

Article 83. The power to administer national finances shall be exercised as the Diet shall determine.

Article 84. No new taxes shall be imposed or existing ones modified except by law or under such conditions as law may prescribe.

Article 85. No money shall be expended nor shall the State obligate itself, except as authorized by the Diet.

Article 86. The Cabinet shall prepare and submit to the Diet for its consideration and decision a budget for each fiscal year.

Article 87. In order to provide for unforeseen deficiencies in the budget, a reserve fund may be authorized by the Diet to be expended upon the responsibility of the Cabinet.

The Cabinet must get subsequent approval of the Diet for all payments from the reserve fund.

Article 88. All property of the Imperial Household shall belong to the State. All expenses of the Imperial Household shall be appropriated by the Diet in the budget.

Article 89. No public money or other property shall be expended or appropriated for the use, benefit or maintenance of any religious institution or association, or for any charitable, educational or benevolent enterprises not under the control of public authority.

Article 90. Final accounts of the expenditures and revenues of the State shall be audited annually by a Board of Audit and submitted by the Cabinet to the Diet, together with the statement of audit, during the fiscal year immediately following the period covered.

The organization and competency of the Board of Audit shall be determined by law.

Article 91. At regular intervals and at least annually, the Cabinet shall report to the Diet and the people on the state of national finances.

CHAPTER VIII: LOCAL SELF-GOVERNMENT

Article 92. Regulations concerning organization and operations of local public entities shall be fixed by law in accordance with the principle of local autonomy.

Article 93. The local public entities shall establish assemblies as their deliberative organs, in accordance with law.

The chief executive officers of all local public entities, the members of their assemblies, and such other local officials as may be determined by law shall be elected by direct popular vote within their several communities.

Article 94. Local public entities shall have the right to manage their property, affairs and administration and to enact their own regulations within law.

Article 95. A special law, applicable only to one local public entity, cannot be enacted by the Diet without the consent of the majority of the voters of the local public entity concerned, obtained in accordance with law.

CHAPTER XI: AMENDMENTS

Article 96. Amendments to this Constitution shall be initiated by the Diet, through a concurring vote of two-thirds or more of all the members of each House and shall thereupon be submitted to the people for ratification, which shall require the affirmative vote of a majority of all votes cast thereon, at a special referendum or at such election as the Diet shall specify.

Amendments when so ratified shall immediately be promulgated by the Emperor in the name of the people, as an integral part of this Constitution.

CHAPTER X: SUPREME LAW

Article 97. The fundamental human rights by this Constitution guaranteed to the people of Japan are fruits of the age-old struggle of man to be free; they have survived the many exacting tests for durability and are conferred upon this and future generations in trust, to be held for all time inviolate.

Article 98. This Constitution shall be the supreme law of the nation and no law, ordinance, imperial rescript or other act of government, or part thereof, contrary to the provisions hereof shall have legal force or validity.

The treaties concluded by Japan and established laws of nations shall be faithfully observed.

Article 99. The Emperor or the Regent as well as Ministers of State, members of the Diet, judges, and all other public officials have the obligation to respect and uphold this Constitution.

CHAPTER XI: SUPPLEMENTARY PROVISIONS

Article 100. This Constitution shall be enforced as from the day when the period of six months will have elapsed counting from the day of its promulgation.

The enactment of laws necessary for the enforcement of this Constitution, the election of members of the House of Councillors and the procedure for the convocation of the Diet and other preparatory procedures necessary for the enforcement of this Constitution may be executed before the day prescribed in the preceding paragraph.

Article 101. If the House of Councillors is not constituted before the effective date of this Constitution, the House of Representatives shall function as the Diet until such time as the House of Councillors shall be constituted.

Article 102. The term of office for half the members of the House of Councillors serving in the first term under this Constitution shall be three years. Members falling under this category shall be determined in accordance with law.

Article 103. The Ministers of State, members of the House of Representatives and judges in office on the effective date of this Constitution, and all other public officials who occupy positions corresponding to such positions as are recognized by this Constitution shall not forfeit their positions automatically on account of the enforcement of this Constitution unless otherwise specified by law. When, however, successors are elected or appointed under the provisions of this Constitution, they shall forfeit their position as a matter of course.

Sources

CHAPTER 1

DIMOCK, MARSHALL E., *The Japanese Technocracy*, New York: Walker/Weatherhill, 1968.
INSTITUTE OF ADMINISTRATIVE MANAGEMENT (Tokyo, Japan), "The Organization of the Government of Japan", September, 1983.
INSTITUTE OF ADMINISTRATIVE MANAGEMENT (Tokyo, Japan), "The Structure of Public Administration in Japan", Public Administration Series No. 2, March, 1983.
JOHNSON, CHALMERS, *MITI and the Japanese Miracle: The Growth of Industrial Policy, 1925–1975*, Stanford, California: Stanford University Press, 1982.
MCNELLY, THEODORE, *Politics and Government in Japan*, Boston: Haughton, Mifflin Co., 1972.
MINISTRY OF HOME AFFAIRS LOCAL AUTONOMY COLLEGE (Tokyo, Japan). "Election System in Japan", 1985.
"Public Administration in Japan", edited by the Tokyo Roundtable Organizing Committee, International Institute of Administrative Sciences, Tokyo, Japan, 1982.
UKAI, NOBUSHIGE, "Constitutional Trends and Developments", *Annals of the American Academy of Political and Social Sciences*, Vol. 308, November, 1956, pp. 1–9.
VALEO, FRANCIS R., AND MORRISON, CHARLES E., *The Japanese Diet and the US Congress*, Boulder, Colorado: Westview Press, 1983.
VOGEL, EZRA F., *Japan as Number 1: Lessons for America*, Cambridge, Mass.: Harvard University Press, 1979.
VOGEL, EZRA F., *Modern Japanese Organization and Decision-Making*, Los Angeles: University of California Press, 1975.
WARD, ROBERT E., *Japan's Political System*, Englewood Cliffs, New Jersey: Prentice-Hall, Inc., 1978.

CHAPTER 2

DIMOCK, MARSHALL E., *The Japanese Technocracy*, New York: Walker/Weatherhill, 1968.
FUKUI, HARUHIRO, "Japan's Nakasone Government", *Current History: a World Affairs Journal*, November, 1983.
INSTITUTE OF ADMINISTRATIVE MANAGEMENT (Tokyo, Japan), "Administrative Management in Japan", Public Administration Series No. 1, March, 1982.
INSTITUTE OF ADMINISTRATIVE MANAGEMENT (Tokyo, Japan), "The Organization of the Government of Japan", September, 1983.

INSTITUTE OF ADMINISTRATIVE MANAGEMENT (Tokyo, Japan), "The Structure of Public Administration in Japan", Public Administration Series No. 2, March, 1983.
MCNELLY, THEODORE, *Politics and Government in Japan*, Boston: Houghton, Mifflin Co., 1972.
NAKASONE, YASUHIRO, "Administrative Reform: The Greatest Challenge in Postwar History", speech copied from unknown source.
"Public Administration in Japan", edited by the Tokyo Roundtable Organizing Committee, International Institute of Administrative Sciences, Tokyo, Japan, 1982.
VALEO, FRANCIS R., AND MORRISON, CHARLES E., *The Japanese Diet and the U.S. Congress*, Boulder, Colorado: Westview Press, 1983.
WARD, ROBERT E., *Japan's Political System*, Englewood Cliffs, NJ: Prentice-Hall, Inc., 1978.

CHAPTER 3

THE ADMINISTRATIVE MANAGEMENT AGENCY, Prime Minister's Office, Government of Japan, "Administrative Reform in Japan", 1982.
DRUCKER, PETER F., "Economic Realities and Enterprise Strategy", *Modern Japanese Organizations and Decision-Making*, pp. 228–36, Berkley, California: University of California Press, 1975.
"Government Deficit-Covering Bonds Should Go", editorial, *Japan Times*, July 17, 1984.
HASHIMOTO, TOHEU, "On the Local Tax System — Choice and Burden", *Local Government Review in Japan*, No. 11, 1983, edited by the Jichi Sogo Center, Tokyo, Japan.
INSTITUTE OF ADMINISTRATIVE MANAGEMENT (Tokyo, Japan), "The Fifth Report on Administrative Reform", the final report of the Provisional Commission on Administrative Reform, March, 1984.
MINISTRY OF FINANCE, BUDGET BUREAU, "*The Budget in Brief — Japan*", 1984.
OGITA, TAMOTSU, "The Fixed Rate Reduction of National Government Disbursements", *Local Government Review in Japan*, No. 13, 1985, edited by the Jichi Sogo Center, Tokyo, Japan.
SHIBATA, TOKUE, ed., *Public Finance in Japan*, Tokyo: University of Tokyo Press, 1986.
WRIGHT, DEIL S., "Administrative Reform in Japan: Politics, Policy, and Public Administration in a Deliberative Society", unpublished draft.

CHAPTER 4

HASHIMOTO, TOKRU, "On the Local Tax System — Choice and Burden", *Local Government Review in Japan*, No. 11, 1983, edited by the Jichi Sogo Center, Tokyo, Japan.

INSTITUTE OF ADMINISTRATIVE MANAGEMENT (Tokyo, Japan), "The Fifth Report on Administrative Reform", the final report of the Provisional Commission on Administrative Reform, March,1984.
INSTITUTE OF ADMINISTRATIVE MANAGEMENT (Tokyo, Japan), "The Organization of the Government of Japan", September, 1983.
ISHIHARA, NOBUO, "The Security of Financial Sources and Local Autonomy", *Local Government Review in Japan*, No. 12, 1984, edited by the Jichi Sogo Center, Tokyo, Japan.
MINISTRY OF FINANCE, BUDGET BUREAU, "*The Budget in Brief — Japan*", 1984.
"Public Administration in Japan", edited by the Tokyo Roundtable Organizing Committee of the International Institute of Administrative Sciences, Tokyo, Japan, 1982.
SHIKATA, TOKUE, ed., *Public Finance in Japan*, Tokyo: University of Tokyo Press, 1986.
THUROW, LESTER, *The Zero-Sum Society: Distribution and the Possibilities for Economic Change*, New York: Basic Books, 1980.
VALEO, FRANCIS, R., AND MORRISON, CHARLES, E., *The Japanese Diet and the US Congress*, Boulder, Colorado: Westview Press, 1983.
VOGEL, EZRA, F., *Modern Japanese Organization and Decision-Making*, Los Angeles: University of California Press, 1975.

CHAPTER 5

BINGMAN, CHARLES F., "Public Administration in Japan: Japanese Public Sector Productivity and Workforce Management", Washington, DC: Occasional paper published by the US National Academy of Public Administration, December, 1984.
DIMOCK, MARSHALL E., *The Japanese Technocracy*, New York: Walker/Weatherhill, 1968.
INSTITUTE OF ADMINISTRATIVE MANAGEMENT (Tokyo, Japan), "Administrative Management in Japan", Public Administration Series No. 1, March, 1982.
"Local Autonomy Law", Tokyo: Jichi Sogo Center, 1986.
"Local Government and Regional Development in Japan", Tokyo: Jichi Sogo Center, April, 1985.
"Local Public Administration in Japan", Tokyo: Jichi Sogo Center, April, 1984.
REED, STEVEN R., *Japanese Prefectures and Policymaking*, Pittsburgh, Pa. University of Pittsburgh Press, 1986.
SHINDO, MUNEYUKI, "Relations Between National Government and Local Government in Japan", article; publisher unknown.

CHAPTER 6

BINGMAN, CHARLES F., "Public Administration in Japan: Japanese Public Sector Productivity and Workforce Management", Washington, DC: occasional paper published by the US National Academy of Public Administration, December, 1984.

ENDO, FUMIO, "The Direction of Local Autonomy After the Second Ad Hoc Commission's Report on Administrative Reform", *Local Government Review in Japan*, No.12, 1984, edited by the Jichi Sogo Center, Tokyo, Japan.

INSTITUTE OF ADMINISTRATIVE MANAGEMENT (Tokyo, Japan), "The Structure of Public Administration in Japan", Public Administration Series No. 2, March, 1983.

KATAYAMA, TORANOSUKE, "The Present Situation and Theme of Administrative Reform of Local Public Entities", *Local Government Review in Japan*, No. 13, 1985, edited by the Jichi Sogo Center.

"Local Autonomy Law", Tokyo: Jichi Sogo Center, 1986.

"Local Public Adminstration in Japan", Tokyo: Jichi Sogo Center, April, 1984.

"Local Public Enterprise System in Japan", Tokyo: Jichi Sogo Center, February, 1984.

"Public Administration in Japan", edited by the Tokyo Roundtable Organizing Committee of the International Institute of Administrative Sciences, Tokyo, Japan, 1982.

"Statistical Abstract of Japanese Local Government", Tokyo: Jichi Sogo Center, November, 1985.

CHAPTER 7

"Government Deficit-Covering Bonds Should Go", Editorial, Japan Times, July 17, 1984.

HASHIMOTO, TOHRU, "On the Local Tax System — Choice and Burden", *Local Government Review in Japan*, No. 11, 1983, edited by the Jichi Sogo Center, Tokyo, Japan.

ISHIHARA, NOBUO, "A Trying Time for Local Finance", *Local Government Review in Japan*, No. 11, 1983, edited by the Jichi Sogo Center, Tokyo, Japan.

ISHIHARA, NOBUO, "The Security of Financial Sources and Local Autonomy", *Local Government Review in Japan*, No. 12, 1984, edited by the Jichi Sogo Center, Tokyo, Japan.

"Local Government and Regional Development in Japan", Tokyo: Jichi Sogo Center, February, 1985.

"Local Public Finance in Japan", Tokyo: Jichi Sogo Center, February, 1982.

"Local Tax System in Japan", Tokyo: Jichi Sogo Center, August, 1984.

KATAYAMA, TORANOSUKE, "The Present Situation and Theme of Administrative Reform of Local Public Entities", *Local Government Review in Japan*, No. 13, 1985, edited by the Jichi Sogo Center, Tokyo, Japan.

MINISTRY OF FINANCE, BUDGET BUREAU, *The Budget in Brief —
Japan*", 1984.
OGITA, TAMOTSU, "The Fixed-rate Reduction of National Government
Disbursements", *Local Government Review in Japan*, No. 13, 1985, edited
by the Jichi Sogo Center, Tokyo, Japan.
SHITAKA, TOKUE, ed., *Public Finance in Japan*, Tokyo: University of
Tokyo Press, 1986.
"Statistical Abstract of Japanese Local Government", Tokyo: Jichi Sogo
Center, November, 1985.

CHAPTER 8

DIMOCK, MARSHALL E., *The Japanese Technocracy*, New York:
Walker/Weatherhill, 1968.
"The Fifth Report on Administrative Reform", the final report of the
Provisional Commission on Administrative Reform, Tokyo: The Institute of
Administrative Management, March, 1984.
JOHNSON, CHALMERS, *MITI and the Japanese Miracle: The Growth of
Industrial Policy, 1925–1975*, Stanford, California: Stanford University
Press, 1982.
"Local Autonomy Law", Tokyo: Jichi Sogo Center, 1986.
"Local Government and Regional Development in Japan", Tokyo: Jichi
Sogo Center, February, 1985.
"Local Public Administration in Japan", Tokyo: Jichi Sogo Center, 1984.
OKIMOTO, DANIEL I. ed., *Japan's Economy: Coping with Change in the
International Environment*, Boulder, Colorado: Westview Press, 1982.
"The Organization of the Government of Japan", Tokyo: Institute of
Administrative Management, September, 1983.
REED, STEVEN R., *Japanese Prefectures and Policymaking*, Pittsburgh,
Pa.: University of Pittsburgh Press, 1986.
VOGEL, EZRA, *Japan as Number 1: Lessons for America*, Cambridge,
Mass.: Harvard University Press, 1979.
VOGEL, EZRA, *Modern Japanese Organization and Decision-Making*, Los
Angeles: University of California Press, 1975.

CHAPTER 9

BINGMAN, CHARLES F., "Public Administration in Japan: Japanese
Public Sector Productivity and Workforce Management", Washington, DC:
occasional paper published by the National Academy of Public Administra-
tion, December, 1984.
"The Fifth Report on Administrative Reform", the final report of the
Provisional Commission on Administrative Reform, Tokyo: Institute of
Administrative Management, March, 1984.
"Local Public Enterprise System in Japan", Tokyo: Jichi Sogo Center,
February, 1984.

JOHNSON, CHALMERS, *MITI and the Japanese Miracle: The Growth of Industrial Policy, 1925–1975,* Stanford, California:, Stanford University Press, 1982.
"The Organization of the Government of Japan", Tokyo: Institute of Administrative Management, September, 1983.

CHAPTER 10

"Education System in Japan", Tokyo: Jichi Sogo Center, February, 1984.
"Local Autonomy Law", Tokyo: Jichi Sogo Center, 1986.
"Local Public Administration in Japan", Tokyo: Jichi Sogo Center, April, 1984.
"The Organization of the Government of Japan", Tokyo: Institute of Administrative Management, September, 1983.
REED, STEVEN R., *Japanese Prefectures and Policymaking*, Pittsburgh, Pa.: University of Pittsburgh Press, 1986.
REISCHAUER, EDWIN O., *The Japanese*, Cambridge, Mass.: Harvard University Press, 1978.
SHINDO, MUNEYUKI, *Relations Between National Government and Local Government in Japan*" (publisher and date not known).
VOGEL, EZRA, *Japan as Number 1: Lessons for America*, Cambridge, Mass.: Harvard University Press, 1979.

CHAPTER 11

"Administrative Management in Japan", Tokyo: Institute of Administrative Management, Public Administration Series No. 1, March, 1982.
BINGMAN, CHARLES F., "Public Administration in Japan: Japanese Public Sector Productivity and Workforce Management", Washington, DC: occasional paper published by the National Academy of Public Administration, December, 1984.
"The Fifth Report on Administrative Reform", the final report of the Provisional Commission on Administrative Reform, Tokyo: Institute of Administrative Management, March, 1984.
"The Local Public Enterprise System in Japan", Tokyo: Jichi Sogo Center, February, 1984.
"The Organization of the Government of Japan", Tokyo: Institute of Administrative Management, September, 1983.
NAKASONE, YASUHIRO, "Administrative Reform: The Greatest Challenge in Postwar History", speech copied from unknown source.
"Statistical Abstract of Japanese Local Government", Tokyo: Jichi Sogo Center, November, 1985.
WRIGHT, DEIL S., "Administrative Reform in Japan: Politics, Policy, and Public Administration in a Deliberative Society", unpublished draft.

CHAPTER 12

BINGMAN, CHARLES F., "Public Administration in Japan: Japanese Public Sector Productivity and Workforce Management", Washington, DC: occasional paper published by the National Academy of Public Adminstration, December, 1984.
DIMOCK, MARSHALL E., *The Japanese Technocracy*, New York: Walker/Weatherhill, 1968.
KAGOSHIMA, SHEGEHARU, "Measures to Improve Personnel Administration", *Local Government Review in Japan*, No. 12, 1984, edited by the Jichi Sogo Center.
KAWANAKA, NIHO, "Present Local Government Personnel System and its Problems", *Local Government Review in Japan*, No. 9, 1981, edited by the Local Government Research and Data Center.
JOHNSON, CHALMERS, *"MITI and the Japanese Miracle: The Growth of Industrial Policy, 1925–1975*, Stanford, California: Stanford University Press, 1982.
Local Government Review in Japan, edited by the Local Government Research and Data Centre, Tokyo, Japan.
"Local Public Service Personnel System in Japan", Tokyo: Jichi Sogo Center, February, 1983.
"The Structure of Public Administration in Japan", Tokyo: Institute of Administrative Management, Public Administration Series No. 2, March, 1983.
VOGEL, EZRA, *Japan as Number 1: Lessons for America*, Cambridge, Mass.: Harvard University Press, 1979.

Index